THE OXFORD BOOK
OF ENGLISH VERSE

Milton to Burns

THE OXFORD BOOK OF ENGLISH VERSE

Part 3

Milton to Burns

Chosen and Edited

by

Arthur Quiller-Couch

YESTERDAY'S CLASSICS

ITHACA, NEW YORK

ISBN: 978-1-63334-040-4

Yesterday's Classics, LLC
PO Box 339
Ithaca, NY 14851

TO

THE PRESIDENT

FELLOWS AND SCHOLARS

OF

TRINITY COLLEGE OXFORD

A HOUSE OF LEARNING

ANCIENT LIBERAL HUMANE

AND MY MOST KINDLY NURSE

PREFACE

FOR this Anthology I have tried to range over the whole field of English Verse from the beginning, or from the Thirteenth Century to this closing year of the Nineteenth, and to choose the best. Nor have I sought in these Islands only, but wheresoever the Muse has followed the tongue which among living tongues she most delights to honour. To bring home and render so great a spoil compendiously has been my capital difficulty. It is for the reader to judge if I have so managed it as to serve those who already love poetry and to implant that love in some young minds not yet initiated.

My scheme is simple. I have arranged the poets as nearly as possible in order of birth, with such groupings of anonymous pieces as seemed convenient. For convenience, too, as well as to avoid a dispute-royal, I have gathered the most of the Ballads into the middle of the Seventeenth Century; where they fill a languid interval between two winds of inspiration—the Italian dying down with Milton and the French following at the heels of the restored Royalists. For convenience, again, I have set myself certain rules of spelling. In the very earliest poems inflection and spelling are structural, and to modernize is to destroy. But as old inflections fade into modern the old spelling becomes less and less vital, and has been brought (not, I hope, too abruptly) into line with that sanctioned by use and familiar. To do this seemed wiser than to discourage many readers for the sake of diverting others by a scent of antiquity which—to be essential—should breathe of something rarer than an odd arrangement of type. But there are scholars whom I cannot expect to agree with me; and to conciliate them I have excepted Spenser and Milton from the rule.

Glosses of archaic and otherwise difficult words are given at the foot of the page: but the text has not been disfigured with reference-marks. And rather than make the book unwieldy I have eschewed notes— reluctantly when some obscure passage or allusion seemed to ask for a timely word; with more equanimity when the temptation was to criticize or 'appreciate.' For the function of the anthologist includes criticizing in silence.

Care has been taken with the texts. But I have sometimes thought it consistent with the aim of the book to prefer the more beautiful to the better attested reading. I have often excised weak or superfluous stanzas when sure that excision would improve; and have not hesitated to extract a few stanzas from a long poem when persuaded that they could stand alone as a lyric. The apology for such experiments can only lie in their success: but the risk is one which, in my judgement, the anthologist ought to take. A few small corrections have been made, but only when they were quite obvious.

The numbers chosen are either lyrical or epigram-matic. Indeed I am mistaken if a single epigram included fails to preserve at least some faint thrill of the emotion through which it had to pass before the Muse's lips let it fall, with however exquisite deliberation. But the lyrical spirit is volatile and notoriously hard to bind with definitions; and seems to grow wilder with the years. With the anthologist—as with the fisherman who knows the fish at the end of his sea-line—the gift, if he have it, comes by sense, improved by practice. The definition, if he be clever enough to frame one, comes by after-thought. I don't know that it helps, and am sure that it may easily mislead.

Having set my heart on choosing the best, I resolved not to be dissuaded by common objections against anthologies—that they repeat one another until the proverb δὶς ἢ τρὶς τὰ καλά loses all application—or perturbed if my judgement should often agree with that of good critics. The best is the best, though a hundred judges have declared it so; nor had it been any feat to search out and insert the second-rate merely because it happened to be recondite. To be sure, a man must come to such a task as mine haunted by his youth and the favourites he loved in days when he had much enthusiasm but little reading.

> A deeper import
> Lurks in the legend told my infant years
> Than lies upon that truth we live to learn.

Few of my contemporaries can erase—or would wish to erase—the dye their minds took from the late Mr. Palgrave's *Golden Treasury:* and he who has returned to it again and again with an affection born of companionship on many journeys must remember not only what the *Golden Treasury* includes, but the moment when this or that poem appealed to him, and even how it lies on the page. To Mr. Bullen's *Lyrics from the Elizabethan Song Books* and his other treasuries I own a more advised debt. Nor am I free of obligation to anthologies even more recent—to Archbishop Trench's *Household Book of Poetry*, Mr. Locker-Lampson's *Lyra Elegantiarum*, Mr. Miles' *Poets and Poetry of the Century*, Mr. Beeching's *Paradise of English Poetry*, Mr. Henley's *English Lyrics*, Mrs. Sharp's *Lyra Celtica*, Mr. Yeats' *Book of Irish Verse*, and Mr. Churton Collins' *Treasury of Minor British Poetry*: though my rule has been to consult these after making my own choice. Yet I can claim that the help derived from them—though gratefully owned—bears but a trifling proportion to the labour, special and desultory, which has gone to the making of my book.

For the anthologist's is not quite the *dilettante* business for which it is too often and ignorantly derided. I say this, and immediately repent; since my wish is that the reader should in his own pleasure quite forget the editor's labour, which too has been pleasant: that, standing aside, I may believe this book has made the Muses' access easier when, in the right hour, they come to him to uplift or to console—

ἄκλητος μὲν ἔγωγε μένοιμί κεν· ἐς δὲ καλεύντων θαρσήσας Μοίσαισι σὺν ἀμετέραισιν ἱκοίμαν.

October 1900   A.T.Q.C.

NUMBER	CONTENTS		PAGE

NUMBER	CONTENTS		PAGE

NUMBER	CONTENTS		PAGE

JOHN MILTON

1608–1674

307.   *Hymn on the Morning*
            of Christ's Nativity

IT was the Winter wilde,
    While the Heav'n-born-childe,
        All meanly wrapt in the rude manger lies;
Nature in aw to him
Had doff't her gawdy trim,
        With her great Master so to sympathize:
It was no season then for her
To wanton with the Sun her lusty Paramour.

Only with speeches fair
She woo's the gentle Air
        To hide her guilty front with innocent Snow,
And on her naked shame,
Pollute with sinfull blame,
        The Saintly Vail of Maiden white to throw,
Confounded, that her Makers eyes
Should look so neer upon her foul deformities.

But he her fears to cease,
Sent down the meek-eyd Peace,
        She crown'd with Olive green, came softly sliding
Down through the turning sphear
His ready Harbinger,
        With Turtle wing the amorous clouds dividing,
And waving wide her mirtle wand,
She strikes a universall Peace through Sea and Land.

1

No War, or Battails sound
Was heard the World around,
    The idle spear and shield were high up hung;
The hookéd Chariot stood
Unstain'd with hostile blood,
    The Trumpet spake not to the arméd throng,
And Kings sate still with awfull eye,
As if they surely knew their sovran Lord was by.

But peacefull was the night
Wherin the Prince of light
    His raign of peace upon the earth began:
The Windes with wonder whist,
Smoothly the waters kist,
    Whispering new joyes to the milde Ocean,
Who now hath quite forgot to rave,
While Birds of Calm sit brooding on the charméd wave.

The Stars with deep amaze
Stand fixt in stedfast gaze,
    Bending one way their pretious influence,
And will not take their flight,
For all the morning light,
    Or Lucifer that often warn'd them thence;
But in their glimmering Orbs did glow,
Untill their Lord himself bespake, and bid them go.

And though the shady gloom
Had given day her room,
    The Sun himself with-held his wonted speed,
And hid his head for shame,
As his inferiour flame,
    The new enlightn'd world no more should need;
He saw a greater Sun appear
Then his bright Throne, or burning Axletree could bear.

The Shepherds on the Lawn,
Or ere the point of dawn,

Sate simply chatting in a rustick row;
Full little thought they than,
That the mighty Pan
  Was kindly com to live with them below;
Perhaps their loves, or els their sheep,
Was all that did their silly thoughts so busie keep.

When such musick sweet
Their hearts and ears did greet,
  As never was by mortall finger strook,
Divinely-warbled voice
Answering the stringéd noise,
  As all their souls in blisfull rapture took:
The Air such pleasure loth to lose,
With thousand echo's still prolongs each heav'nly close.

Nature that heard such sound
Beneath the hollow round
  Of Cynthia's seat, the Airy region thrilling,
Now was almost won
To think her part was don,
  And that her raign had here its last fulfilling;
She knew such harmony alone
Could hold all Heav'n and Earth in happier union.

At last surrounds their sight
A Globe of circular light,
  That with long beams the shame-fac't night array'd,
The helméd Cherubim
And sworded Seraphim,
  Are seen in glittering ranks with wings displaid,
Harping in loud and solemn quire,
With unexpressive notes to Heav'ns new-born Heir.

Such musick (as 'tis said)
Before was never made,
  But when of old the sons of morning sung,
While the Creator Great

His constellations set,
    And the well-ballanc't world on hinges hung,
And cast the dark foundations deep,
And bid the weltring waves their oozy channel keep.

Ring out ye Crystall sphears,
Once bless our human ears,
    (If ye have power to touch our senses so)
And let your silver chime
Move in melodious time;
    And let the Base of Heav'ns deep Organ blow
And with your ninefold harmony
Make up full consort to th' Angelike symphony.

For if such holy Song
Enwrap our fancy long,
    Time will run back, and fetch the age of gold,
And speckl'd vanity
Will sicken soon and die,
    And leprous sin will melt from earthly mould,
And Hell it self will pass away,
And leave her dolorous mansions to the peering day.

Yea Truth, and Justice then
Will down return to men,
    Th' enameld Arras of the Rain-bow wearing,
And Mercy set between,
Thron'd in Celestiall sheen,
    With radiant feet the tissued clouds down stearing,
And Heav'n as at som festivall,
Will open wide the Gates of her high Palace Hall.

But wisest Fate sayes no,
This must not yet be so,
    The Babe lies yet in smiling Infancy,
That on the bitter cross
Must redeem our loss;
    So both himself and us to glorifie:

Yet first to those ychain'd in sleep,
The wakefull trump of doom must thunder through the deep,

With such a horrid clang
As on mount Sinai rang
    While the red fire, and smouldring clouds out brake:
The agéd Earth agast
With terrour of that blast,
    Shall from the surface to the center shake;
When at the worlds last session,
The dreadfull Judge in middle Air shall spread his throne.

And then at last our bliss
Full and perfect is,
    But now begins; for from this happy day
Th' old Dragon under ground
In straiter limits bound,
    Not half so far casts his usurpéd sway,
And wrath to see his Kingdom fail,
Swindges the scaly Horrour of his foulded tail.

The Oracles are dumm,
No voice or hideous humm
    Runs through the archéd roof in words deceiving.
Apollo from his shrine
Can no more divine,
    With hollow shreik the steep of Delphos leaving.
No nightly trance, or breathéd spell,
Inspire's the pale-ey'd Priest from the prophetic cell.

The lonely mountains o're,
And the resounding shore,
    A voice of weeping heard, and loud lament;
From haunted spring, and dale
Edg'd with poplar pale,
    The parting Genius is with sighing sent,
With flowre-inwov'n tresses torn
The Nimphs in twilight shade of tangled thickets mourn.

In consecrated Earth,
And on the holy Hearth,
    The Lars, and Lemures moan with midnight plaint,
In Urns, and Altars round,
A drear, and dying sound
    Affrights the Flamins at their service quaint;
And the chill Marble seems to sweat,
While each peculiar power forgoes his wonted seat.

Peor, and Baalim,
Forsake their Temples dim,
    With that twise-batter'd god of Palestine,
And moonéd Ashtaroth,
Heav'ns Queen and Mother both,
    Now sits not girt with Tapers holy shine,
The Libyc Hammon shrinks his horn,
In vain the Tyrian Maids their wounded Thamuz mourn.

And sullen Moloch fled,
Hath left in shadows dred,
    His burning Idol all of blackest hue,
In vain with Cymbals ring,
They call the grisly king,
    In dismall dance about the furnace blue;
The brutish gods of Nile as fast,
Isis and Orus, and the Dog Anubis hast.

Nor is Osiris seen
In Memphian Grove, or Green,
    Trampling the unshowr'd Grasse with lowings loud:
Nor can he be at rest
Within his sacred chest,
    Naught but profoundest Hell can be his shroud,
In vain with Timbrel'd Anthems dark
The sable-stoléd Sorcerers bear his worshipt Ark.

He feels from Juda's Land
The dredded Infants hand,

The rayes of Bethlehem blind his dusky eyn;
Nor all the gods beside,
Longer dare abide,
    Not Typhon huge ending in snaky twine:
Our Babe to shew his Godhead true,
Can in his swadling bands controul the damnéd crew.

So when the Sun in bed,
Curtain'd with cloudy red,
    Pillows his chin upon an Orient wave,
The flocking shadows pale,
Troop to th' infernall jail,
    Each fetter'd Ghost slips to his severall grave,
And the yellow-skirted Fayes,
Fly after the Night-steeds, leaving their Moon-lov'd maze.

But see the Virgin blest,
Hath laid her Babe to rest.
    Time is our tedious Song should here have ending,
Heav'ns youngest teeméd Star,
Hath fixt her polisht Car,
    Her sleeping Lord with Handmaid Lamp attending:
And all about the Courtly Stable,
Bright-harnest Angels sit in order serviceable.

308. *On Time*

FLY envious Time, till thou run out thy race,
    Call on the lazy leaden-stepping hours,
Whose speed is but the heavy Plummets pace;
And glut thy self with what thy womb devours,
Which is no more then what is false and vain,
And meerly mortal dross;
So little is our loss,
So little is thy gain.
For when as each thing bad thou hast entomb'd,
And last of all, thy greedy self consum'd,

7

Then long Eternity shall greet our bliss
With an individual kiss;
And Joy shall overtake us as a flood,
When every thing that is sincerely good
And perfectly divine,
With Truth, and Peace, and Love shall ever shine
About the supreme Throne
Of him, t'whose happy-making sight alone,
When once our heav'nly-guided soul shall clime,
Then all this Earthy grosnes quit,
Attir'd with Stars, we shall for ever sit,
    Triumphing over Death, and Chance, and thee O Time.

309.   *At a Solemn Musick*

BLEST pair of Sirens, pledges of Heav'ns joy,
    Sphear-born harmonious Sisters, Voice, and Vers,
Wed your divine sounds, and mixt power employ
Dead things with inbreath'd sense able to pierce,
And to our high-rais'd phantasie present,
That undisturbéd Song of pure content,
Ay sung before the saphire-colour'd throne
To him that sits theron
With Saintly shout, and solemn Jubily,
Where the bright Seraphim in burning row
Their loud up-lifted Angel trumpets blow,
And the Cherubick host in thousand quires
Touch their immortal Harps of golden wires,
With those just Spirits that wear victorious Palms,
Hymns devout and holy Psalms
Singing everlastingly;
That we on Earth with undiscording voice
May rightly answer that melodious noise;
As once we did, till disproportion'd sin
Jarr'd against natures chime, and with harsh din
Broke the fair musick that all creatures made

To their great Lord, whose love their motion sway'd
In perfect Diapason, whilst they stood
In first obedience, and their state of good.
O may we soon again renew that Song,
And keep in tune with Heav'n, till God ere long
To his celestial consort us unite,
To live with him, and sing in endles morn of light.

310. *L'Allegro*

HENCE loathéd Melancholy
   Of Cerberus and blackest midnight born,
In Stygian Cave forlorn
   'Mongst horrid shapes, and shreiks, and sights unholy.
Find out som uncouth cell,
   Where brooding darknes spreads his jealous wings,
And the night-Raven sings;
   There, under Ebon shades, and low-brow'd Rocks,
As ragged as thy Locks,
   In dark Cimmerian desert ever dwell.
But com thou Goddes fair and free,
In Heav'n ycleap'd Euphrosyne,
And by men, heart-easing Mirth,
Whom lovely Venus, at a birth
With two sister Graces more
To Ivy-crownéd Bacchus bore;
Or whether (as som Sager sing)
The frolick Wind that breathes the Spring,
Zephir with Aurora playing,
As he met her once a Maying,
There on Beds of Violets blew,
And fresh-blown Roses washt in dew,
Fill'd her with thee a daughter fair,
So bucksom, blith, and debonair.
   Haste thee nymph, and bring with thee
Jest and youthful Jollity,

Quips and Cranks, and wanton Wiles,
Nods, and Becks, and Wreathéd Smiles,
Such as hang on Hebe's cheek,
And love to live in dimple sleek;
Sport that wrincled Care derides,
And Laughter holding both his sides.
Com, and trip it as ye go
On the light fantastick toe,
And in thy right hand lead with thee,
The Mountain Nymph, sweet Liberty;
And if I give thee honour due,
Mirth, admit me of thy crue
To live with her, and live with thee,
In unreprovéd pleasures free;
To hear the Lark begin his flight,
And singing startle the dull night,
From his watch-towre in the skies,
Till the dappled dawn doth rise;
Then to com in spight of sorrow,
And at my window bid good morrow,
Through the Sweet-Briar, or the Vine,
Or the twisted Eglantine.
While the Cock with lively din,
Scatters the rear of darknes thin,
And to the stack, or the Barn dore,
Stoutly struts his Dames before,
Oft list'ning how the Hounds and horn
Chearly rouse the slumbring morn,
From the side of som Hoar Hill,
Through the high wood echoing shrill.
Som time walking not unseen
By Hedge-row Elms, on Hillocks green,
Right against the Eastern gate,
Wher the great Sun begins his state,
Rob'd in flames, and Amber light,
The clouds in thousand Liveries dight.

While the Plowman neer at hand,
Whistles ore the Furrow'd Land,
And the Milkmaid singeth blithe,
And the Mower whets his sithe,
And every Shepherd tells his tale
Under the Hawthorn in the dale.
Streit mine eye hath caught new pleasures
Whilst the Lantskip round it measures,
Russet Lawns, and Fallows Gray,
Where the nibling flocks do stray,
Mountains on whose barren brest
The labouring clouds do often rest:
Meadows trim with Daisies pide,
Shallow Brooks, and Rivers wide.
Towers, and Battlements it sees
Boosom'd high in tufted Trees,
Wher perhaps som beauty lies,
The Cynosure of neighbouring eyes.
Hard by, a Cottage chimney smokes,
From betwixt two agéd Okes,
Where Corydon and Thyrsis met,
Are at their savory dinner set
Of Hearbs, and other Country Messes,
Which the neat-handed Phillis dresses;
And then in haste her Bowre she leaves,
With Thestylis to bind the Sheaves;
Or if the earlier season lead
To the tann'd Haycock in the Mead,
Som times with secure delight
The up-land Hamlets will invite,
When the merry Bells ring round,
And the jocond rebecks sound
To many a youth, and many a maid,
Dancing in the Chequer'd shade;
And young and old com forth to play
On a Sunshine Holyday,

11

Till the live-long day-light fail,
Then to the Spicy Nut-brown Ale,
With stories told of many a feat,
How Faery Mab the junkets eat,
She was pincht, and pull'd she sed,
And he by Friars Lanthorn led
Tells how the drudging Goblin swet,
To ern his Cream-bowle duly set,
When in one night, ere glimps of morn,
His shadowy Flale hath thresh'd the Corn
That ten day-labourers could not end,
Then lies him down the Lubbar Fend,
And stretch'd out all the Chimney's length,
Basks at the fire his hairy strength;
And Crop-full out of dores he flings,
Ere the first Cock his Mattin rings.
Thus don the Tales, to bed they creep,
By whispering Windes soon lull'd asleep.
    Towred Cities please us then,
And the busie humm of men,
Where throngs of Knights and Barons bold,
In weeds of Peace high triumphs hold,
With store of Ladies, whose bright eies
Rain influence, and judge the prise
Of Wit, or Arms, while both contend
To win her Grace, whom all commend.
There let Hymen oft appear
In Saffron robe, with Taper clear,
And pomp, and feast, and revelry,
With mask, and antique Pageantry,
Such sights as youthfull Poets dream
On Summer eeves by haunted stream.
Then to the well-trod stage anon,
If Jonsons learnéd Sock be on,
Or sweetest Shakespear fancies childe,
Warble his native Wood-notes wilde,

And ever against eating Cares,
Lap me in soft Lydian Aires,
Married to immortal verse
Such as the meeting soul may pierce
In notes, with many a winding bout
Of linckéd sweetnes long drawn out,
With wanton heed, and giddy cunning,
The melting voice through mazes running;
Untwisting all the chains that ty
The hidden soul of harmony.
That Orpheus self may heave his head
From golden slumber on a bed
Of heapt Elysian flowres, and hear
Such streins as would have won the ear
Of Pluto, to have quite set free
His half regain'd Eurydice.
These delights, if thou canst give,
Mirth with thee, I mean to live.

311. *Il Penseroso*

HENCE, vain deluding joyes,
    The brood of folly without father bred,
How little you bested,
    Or fill the fixéd mind with all your toyes;
Dwell in som idle brain,
    And fancies fond with gaudy shapes possess,
As thick and numberless
    As the gay motes that people the Sun Beams,
Or likest hovering dreams
    The fickle Pensioners of Morpheus train.
But hail thou Goddes, sage and holy,
Hail divinest Melancholy,
Whose Saintly visage is too bright
To hit the Sense of human sight;
And therfore to our weaker view,

Ore laid with black staid Wisdoms hue.
Black, but such as in esteem,
Prince Memnons sister might beseem,
Or that Starr'd Ethiope Queen that strove
To set her beauties praise above
The Sea Nymphs, and their powers offended.
Yet thou art higher far descended,
Thee bright-hair'd Vesta long of yore,
To solitary Saturn bore;
His daughter she (in Saturns raign,
Such mixture was not held a stain)
Oft in glimmering Bowres, and glades
He met her, and in secret shades
Of woody Ida's inmost grove,
Whilst yet there was no fear of Jove.
Com pensive Nun, devout and pure,
Sober, stedfast, and demure,
All in a robe of darkest grain,
Flowing with majestick train,
And sable stole of Cipres Lawn,
Over thy decent shoulders drawn.
Com, but keep thy wonted state,
With eev'n step, and musing gate,
And looks commercing with the skies,
Thy rapt soul sitting in thine eyes:
There held in holy passion still,
Forget thy self to Marble, till
With a sad Leaden downward cast,
Thou fix them on the earth as fast.
And joyn with thee calm Peace, and Quiet,
Spare Fast, that oft with gods doth diet,
And hears the Muses in a ring,
Ay round about Joves Altar sing.
And adde to these retiréd Leasure,
That in trim Gardens takes his pleasure;
But first, and chiefest, with thee bring,

Him that yon soars on golden wing,
Guiding the fiery-wheeléd throne,
The Cherub Contemplation,
And the mute Silence hist along,
'Less Philomel will daign a Song,
In her sweetest, saddest plight,
Smoothing the rugged brow of night,
While Cynthia checks her Dragon yoke,
Gently o're th' accustom'd Oke;
Sweet Bird that shunn'st the noise of folly,
Most musicall, most melancholy!
Thee Chauntress oft the Woods among,
I woo to hear thy eeven-Song;
And missing thee, I walk unseen
On the dry smooth-shaven Green.
To behold the wandring Moon,
Riding neer her highest noon,
Like one that had bin led astray
Through the Heav'ns wide pathles way;
And oft, as if her head she bow'd,
Stooping through a fleecy cloud.
Oft on a Plat of rising ground,
I hear the far-off Curfeu sound,
Over som wide-water'd shoar,
Swinging slow with sullen roar;
Or if the Ayr will not permit,
Som still removéd place will fit,
Where glowing Embers through the room
Teach light to counterfeit a gloom,
Far from all resort of mirth,
Save the Cricket on the hearth,
Or the Belmans drousie charm,
To bless the dores from nightly harm:
Or let my Lamp at midnight hour,
Be seen in som high lonely Towr,
Where I may oft out-watch the Bear,

15

With thrice great Hermes, or unsphear
The spirit of Plato to unfold
What Worlds, or what vast Regions hold
The immortal mind that hath forsook
Her mansion in this fleshly nook:
And of those Dæmons that are found
In fire, air, flood, or under ground,
Whose power hath a true consent
With Planet, or with Element.
Som time let Gorgeous Tragedy
In Scepter'd Pall com sweeping by,
Presenting Thebs, or Pelops line,
Or the tale of Troy divine.
Or what (though rare) of later age,
Ennobléd hath the Buskind stage.
      But, O sad Virgin, that thy power
Might raise Musæus from his bower
Or bid the soul of Orpheus sing
Such notes as warbled to the string,
Drew Iron tears down Pluto's cheek,
And made Hell grant what Love did seek.
Or call up him that left half told
The story of Cambuscan bold,
Of Camball, and of Algarsife,
And who had Canace to wife,
That own'd the vertuous Ring and Glass,
And of the wondrous Hors of Brass,
On which the Tartar King did ride;
And if ought els, great Bards beside,
In sage and solemn tunes have sung,
Of Turneys and of Trophies hung;
Of Forests, and inchantments drear,
Where more is meant then meets the ear.
Thus night oft see me in thy pale career,
Till civil-suited Morn appeer,
Not trickt and frounc't as she was wont,

16

With the Attick Boy to hunt,
But Cherchef't in a comly Cloud,
While rocking Winds are Piping loud,
Or usher'd with a shower still,
When the gust hath blown his fill,
Ending on the russling Leaves,
With minute drops from off the Eaves.
And when the Sun begins to fling
His flaring beams, me Goddes bring
To archéd walks of twilight groves,
And shadows brown that Sylvan loves,
Of Pine, or monumental Oake,
Where the rude Ax with heavéd stroke,
Was never heard the Nymphs to daunt,
Or fright them from their hallow'd haunt.
There in close covert by som Brook,
Where no profaner eye may look,
Hide me from Day's garish eie,
While the Bee with Honied thie,
That at her flowry work doth sing,
And the Waters murmuring
With such consort as they keep,
Entice the dewy-feather'd Sleep;
And let som strange mysterious dream,
Wave at his Wings in Airy stream,
Of lively portrature display'd,
Softly on my eye-lids laid.
And as I wake, sweet musick breath
Above, about, or underneath,
Sent by som spirit to mortals good,
Or th' unseen Genius of the Wood.
    But let my due feet never fail,
To walk the studious Cloysters pale,
And love the high embowéd Roof,
With antick Pillars massy proof,
And storied Windows richly dight,

Casting a dimm religious light.
There let the pealing Organ blow,
To the full voic'd Quire below,
In Service high, and Anthems cleer,
As may with sweetnes, through mine ear,
Dissolve me into extasies,
And bring all Heav'n before mine eyes.
And may at last my weary age
Find out the peacefull hermitage,
The Hairy Gown and Mossy Cell,
Where I may sit and rightly spell
Of every Star that Heav'n doth shew,
And every Herb that sips the dew;
Till old experience do attain
To somthing like Prophetic strain.
These pleasures Melancholy give,
And I with thee will choose to live.

312.   *From 'Arcades'*

O'RE the smooth enameld green
    Where no print of step hath been,
      Follow me as I sing,
      And touch the warbled string.
Under the shady roof
Of branching Elm Star-proof,
      Follow me,
I will bring you where she sits
Clad in splendor as befits
      Her deity.
Such a rural Queen
All Arcadia hath not seen.

From 'Comus'

313.   *i.*

THE Star that bids the Shepherd fold,
  Now the top of Heav'n doth hold,
And the gilded Car of Day,
His glowing Axle doth allay
In the steep Atlantick stream,
And the slope Sun his upward beam
Shoots against the dusky Pole,
Pacing toward the other gole
Of his Chamber in the East.
Mean while welcom Joy, and Feast,
Midnight shout, and revelry,
Tipsie dance, and Jollity.
Braid your Locks with rosie Twine
Dropping odours, dropping Wine.
Rigor now is gon to bed,
And Advice with scrupulous head,
Strict Age, and sowre Severity,
With their grave Saws in slumber ly.
We that are of purer fire
Imitate the Starry Quire,
Who in their nightly watchfull Sphears,
Lead in swift round the Months and Years.
The Sounds, and Seas with all their finny drove
Now to the Moon in wavering Morrice move,
And on the Tawny Sands and Shelves,
Trip the pert Fairies and the dapper Elves;
By dimpled Brook, and Fountain brim,
The Wood-Nymphs deckt with Daisies trim,
Their merry wakes and pastimes keep:
What hath night to do with sleep?
Night hath better sweets to prove,
Venus now wakes, and wak'ns Love . . . . .

Com, knit hands, and beat the ground,
In a light fantastick round.

314.   *ii*

Echo

SWEET Echo, sweetest Nymph that liv'st unseen
        Within thy airy shell
      By slow Meander's margent green,
    And in the violet imbroider'd vale
        Where the love-lorn Nightingale
Nightly to thee her sad Song mourneth well.
Canst thou not tell me of a gentle Pair
        That likest thy Narcissus are?
            O if thou have
        Hid them in som flowry Cave,
          Tell me but where
Sweet Queen of Parly, Daughter of the Sphear!
So maist thou be translated to the skies,
And give resounding grace to all Heav'ns Harmonies!

315.   *iii*

Sabrina

The Spirit sings:

SABRINA fair
    Listen where thou art sitting
Under the glassie, cool, translucent wave,
    In twisted braids of Lillies knitting
The loose train of thy amber-dropping hair,
        Listen for dear honour's sake,
        Goddess of the silver lake,
            Listen and save!
Listen and appear to us,

In name of great Oceanus,
By the earth-shaking Neptune's mace,
And Tethys grave majestick pace,
By hoary Nereus wrincled look,
And the Carpathian wisards hook,
By scaly Tritons winding shell,
And old sooth-saying Glaucus spell,
By Leucothea's lovely hands,
And her son that rules the strands,
By Thetis tinsel-slipper'd feet,
And the Songs of Sirens sweet,
By dead Parthenope's dear tomb,
And fair Ligea's golden comb,
Wherwith she sits on diamond rocks
Sleeking her soft alluring locks,
By all the Nymphs that nightly dance
Upon thy streams with wily glance,
Rise, rise, and heave thy rosie head
From thy coral-pav'n bed,
And bridle in thy headlong wave,
Till thou our summons answered have.
                          Listen and save!

Sabrina replies:

            By the rushy-fringéd bank,
Where grows the Willow and the Osier dank,
            My sliding Chariot stayes,
Thick set with Agat, and the azurn sheen
Of Turkis blew, and Emrauld green
            That in the channell strayes,
Whilst from off the waters fleet
Thus I set my printless feet
O're the Cowslips Velvet head,
            That bends not as I tread,
Gentle swain at thy request
            I am here.

316.   *iv*

The Spirit epiloguizes:

TO the Ocean now I fly,
    And those happy climes that ly
Where day never shuts his eye,
Up in the broad fields of the sky:
There I suck the liquid ayr
All amidst the Gardens fair
Of Hesperus, and his daughters three
That sing about the golden tree:
Along the crispéd shades and bowres
Revels the spruce and jocond Spring,
The Graces, and the rosie-boosom'd Howres,
Thither all their bounties bring,
That there eternal Summer dwels,
And West winds, with musky wing
About the cedar'n alleys fling
Nard, and Cassia's balmy smels.
Iris there with humid bow,
Waters the odorous banks that blow
Flowers of more mingled hew
Than her purfl'd scarf can shew,
And drenches with Elysian dew
(List mortals, if your ears be true)
Beds of Hyacinth, and roses
Where young Adonis oft reposes,
Waxing well of his deep wound
In slumber soft, and on the ground
Sadly sits th' Assyrian Queen;
But far above in spangled sheen
Celestial Cupid her fam'd son advanc't,
Holds his dear Psyche sweet intranc't
After her wandring labours long,
Till free consent the gods among
Make her his eternal Bride,

And from her fair unspotted side
Two blissful twins are to be born,
Youth and Joy; so Jove hath sworn.
　　　But now my task is smoothly don,
I can fly, or I can run
Quickly to the green earths end,
Where the bow'd welkin slow doth bend,
And from thence can soar as soon
To the corners of the Moon.
　　　Mortals that would follow me,
Love vertue, she alone is free.
She can teach ye how to clime
Higher then the Spheary chime;
Or if Vertue feeble were,
Heav'n it self would stoop to her.

317.　　　*Lycidas*

*A Lament for a Friend Drowned in His Passage
from Chester on the Irish Seas, 1637*

YET once more, O ye Laurels, and once more
　　Ye Myrtles brown, with Ivy never-sear,
I com to pluck your Berries harsh and crude,
And with forc'd fingers rude,
Shatter your leaves before the mellowing year.
Bitter constraint, and sad occasion dear,
Compels me to disturb your season due:
For Lycidas is dead, dead ere his prime
Young Lycidas, and hath not left his peer:
Who would not sing for Lycidas? he knew
Himself to sing, and build the lofty rhyme.
He must not flote upon his watry bear
Unwept, and welter to the parching wind,
Without the meed of som melodious tear.
　　　Begin, then, Sisters of the sacred well,

23

That from beneath the seat of Jove doth spring,
Begin, and somwhat loudly sweep the string.
Hence with denial vain, and coy excuse,
So may som gentle Muse
With lucky words favour my destin'd Urn,
And as he passes turn,
And bid fair peace be to my sable shrowd.
For we were nurst upon the self-same hill,
Fed the same flock, by fountain, shade, and rill.

    Together both, ere the high Lawns appear'd
Under the opening eye-lids of the morn,
We drove a field, and both together heard
What time the Gray-fly winds her sultry horn,
Batt'ning our flocks with the fresh dews of night,
Oft till the Star that rose, at Ev'ning, bright
Toward Heav'ns descent had slop'd his westering wheel.
Mean while the Rural ditties were not mute,
Temper'd to th' Oaten Flute;
Rough Satyrs danc'd, and Fauns with clov'n heel,
From the glad sound would not be absent long,
And old Damætas lov'd to hear our song.

    But O the heavy change, now thou art gon,
Now thou art gon, and never must return!
Thee Shepherd, thee the Woods, and desert Caves,
With wilde Thyme and the gadding Vine o'regrown,
And all their echoes mourn.
The Willows, and the Hazle Copses green,
Shall now no more be seen,
Fanning their joyous Leaves to thy soft layes.
As killing as the Canker to the Rose,
Or Taint-worm to the weanling Herds that graze,
Or Frost to Flowers, that their gay wardrop wear,
When first the White thorn blows;
Such, Lycidas, thy loss to Shepherds ear.

    Where were ye Nymphs when the remorseless deep
Clos'd o're the head of your lov'd Lycidas?

For neither were ye playing on the steep,
Where your old Bards, the famous Druids ly,
Nor on the shaggy top of Mona high,
Nor yet where Deva spreads her wisard stream:
Ay me, I fondly dream!
Had ye bin there—for what could that have don?
What could the Muse her self that Orpheus bore,
The Muse her self, for her inchanting son
Whom Universal nature did lament,
When by the rout that made the hideous roar,
His goary visage down the stream was sent,
Down the swift Hebrus to the Lesbian shore.
　　　Alas! what boots it with uncessant care
To tend the homely slighted Shepherds trade,
And strictly meditate the thankles Muse,
Were it not better don as others use,
To sport with Amaryllis in the shade,
Or with the tangles of Neæra's hair?
Fame is the spur that the clear spirit doth raise
(That last infirmity of Noble mind)
To scorn delights, and live laborious dayes;
But the fair Guerdon when we hope to find,
And think to burst out into sudden blaze,
Comes the blind Fury with th' abhorréd shears,
And slits the thin spun life. But not the praise,
Phoebus repli'd, and touch'd my trembling ears;
Fame is no plant that grows on mortal soil,
Nor in the glistering foil
Set off to th' world, nor in broad rumour lies,
But lives and spreds aloft by those pure eyes,
And perfet witnes of all judging Jove;
As he pronounces lastly on each deed,
Of so much fame in Heav'n expect thy meed.
　　　O fountain Arethuse, and thou honour'd floud,
Smooth-sliding Mincius, crown'd with vocall reeds,
That strain I heard was of a higher mood:

But now my Oate proceeds,
And listens to the Herald of the Sea
That came in Neptune's plea,
He ask'd the Waves, and ask'd the Fellon winds,
What hard mishap hath doom'd this gentle swain?
And question'd every gust of rugged wings
That blows from off each beakéd Promontory,
They knew not of his story,
And sage Hippotades their answer brings,
That not a blast was from his dungeon stray'd,
The Ayr was calm, and on the level brine,
Sleek Panope with all her sisters play'd.
It was that fatall and perfidious Bark
Built in th' eclipse, and rigg'd with curses dark,
That sunk so low that sacred head of thine.
        Next Camus, reverend Sire, went footing slow,
His Mantle hairy, and his Bonnet sedge,
Inwrought with figures dim, and on the edge
Like to that sanguine flower inscrib'd with woe.
Ah; Who hath reft (quoth he) my dearest pledge?
Last came, and last did go,
The Pilot of the Galilean lake,
Two massy Keyes he bore of metals twain,
(The Golden opes, the Iron shuts amain)
He shook his Miter'd locks, and stern bespake,
How well could I have spar'd for thee, young swain,
Anow of such as for their bellies sake,
Creep and intrude, and climb into the fold?
Of other care they little reck'ning make,
Then how to scramble at the shearers feast,
And shove away the worthy bidden guest.
Blind mouthes! that scarce themselves know how to hold
A Sheep-hook, or have learn'd ought els the least
That to the faithfull Herdmans art belongs!
What recks it them? What need they? They are sped;
And when they list, their lean and flashy songs

Grate on their scrannel Pipes of wretched straw,
The hungry Sheep look up, and are not fed,
But swoln with wind, and the rank mist they draw,
Rot inwardly, and foul contagion spread:
Besides what the grim Woolf with privy paw
Daily devours apace, and nothing sed,
But that two-handed engine at the door,
Stands ready to smite once, and smite no more.
      Return Alpheus, the dread voice is past,
That shrunk thy streams; Return Sicilian Muse,
And call the Vales, and bid them hither cast
Their Bels, and Flourets of a thousand hues.
Ye valleys low where the milde whispers use,
Of shades and wanton winds, and gushing brooks,
On whose fresh lap the swart Star sparely looks,
Throw hither all your quaint enameld eyes,
That on the green terf suck the honied showres,
And purple all the ground with vernal flowres.
Bring the rathe Primrose that forsaken dies.
The tufted Crow-toe, and pale Gessamine,
The white Pink, and the Pansie freakt with jeat,
The glowing Violet.
The Musk-rose, and the well attir'd Woodbine.
With Cowslips wan that hang the pensive hed,
And every flower that sad embroidery wears:
Bid Amaranthus all his beauty shed,
And Daffadillies fill their cups with tears,
To strew the Laureat Herse where Lycid lies.
For so to interpose a little ease,
Let our frail thoughts dally with false surmise.
Ay me! Whilst thee the shores, and sounding Seas
Wash far away, where ere thy bones are hurld,
Whether beyond the stormy Hebrides,
Where thou perhaps under the whelming tide
Visit'st the bottom of the monstrous world;
Or whether thou to our moist vows deny'd,

Sleep'st by the fable of Bellerus old,
Where the great vision of the guarded Mount
Looks toward Namancos and Bayona's hold;
Look homeward Angel now, and melt with ruth.
And, O ye Dolphins, waft the haples youth.
      Weep no more, woful Shepherds weep no more,
For Lycidas your sorrow is not dead,
Sunk though he be beneath the watry floar,
So sinks the day-star in the Ocean bed,
And yet anon repairs his drooping head,
And tricks his beams, and with new spangled Ore,
Flames in the forehead of the morning sky:
So Lycidas sunk low, but mounted high,
Through the dear might of him that walk'd the waves
Where other groves, and other streams along,
With Nectar pure his oozy Lock's he laves,
And hears the unexpressive nuptiall Song,
In the blest Kingdoms meek of joy and love.
There entertain him all the Saints above,
In solemn troops, and sweet Societies
That sing, and singing in their glory move,
And wipe the tears for ever from his eyes.
Now Lycidas the Shepherds weep no more;
Hence forth thou art the Genius of the shore,
In thy large recompense, and shalt be good
To all that wander in that perilous flood.
      Thus sang the uncouth Swain to th' Okes and rills,
While the still morn went out with Sandals gray,
He touch'd the tender stops of various Quills,
With eager thought warbling his Dorick lay:
And now the Sun had stretch'd out all the hills,
And now was dropt into the Western bay;
At last he rose, and twitch'd his Mantle blew:
To morrow to fresh Woods, and Pastures new.

317.*   *To the Lady Margaret Ley*

DAUGHTER to that good Earl, once President
    Of Englands Council and her Treasury,
  Who liv'd in both, unstain'd with gold or fee,
And left them both, more in himself content,
Till the sad breaking of that Parlament
  Broke him, as that dishonest victory
  At Chæronéa, fatal to liberty,
Kil'd with report that Old man eloquent.
Though later born, then to have known the dayes
  Wherein your father flourisht, yet by you
    Madam, me thinks I see him living yet;
So well your words his noble virtues praise,
  That all both judge you to relate them true,
    And to possess them, Honour'd Margaret.

318.   *On His Blindness*

WHEN I consider how my light is spent
    E're half my days, in this dark world and wide,
  And that one Talent which is death to hide,
Lodg'd with me useless, though my Soul more bent
To serve therewith my Maker, and present
  My true account, least he returning chide,
  Doth God exact day-labour, light deny'd,
I fondly ask; But patience to prevent
That murmur, soon replies, God doth not need
  Either man's work or his own gifts, who best
  Bear his milde yoak, they serve him best, his State
Is Kingly. Thousands at his bidding speed
  And post o're Land and Ocean without rest:
  They also serve who only stand and waite.

319. *To Mr. Lawrence*

L AWRENCE of vertuous Father vertuous Son,
  Now that the Fields are dank, and ways are mire,
  Where shall we sometimes meet, and by the fire
  Help wast a sullen day; what may be won
From the hard Season gaining: time will run
  On smoother, till Favonius re-inspire
  The frozen earth; and cloth in fresh attire
  The Lillie and Rose, that neither sow'd nor spun.
What neat repast shall feast us, light and choice,
  Of Attick tast, with Wine, whence we may rise
  To hear the Lute well toucht, or artfull voice
Warble immortal Notes and Tuskan Ayre?
  He who of those delights can judge, and spare
  To interpose them oft, is not unwise.

320. *To Cyriack Skinner*

C YRIACK, whose Grandsire on the Royal Bench
  Of Brittish Themis, with no mean applause
  Pronounc't and in his volumes taught our Lawes,
  Which others at their Barr so often wrench:
To day deep thoughts resolve with me to drench
  In mirth, that after no repenting drawes;
  Let Euclid rest and Archimedes pause,
  And what the Swede intend, and what the French.
To measure life, learn thou betimes, and know
  Toward solid good what leads the nearest way;
  For other things mild Heav'n a time ordains,
And disapproves that care, though wise in show,
  That with superfluous burden loads the day,
  And when God sends a cheerful hour, refrains.

321. *On His Deceased Wife*

METHOUGHT I saw my late espoused Saint
    Brought to me like Alcestis from the grave,
    Whom Joves great Son to her glad Husband gave,
    Rescu'd from death by force though pale and faint.
Mine as whom washt from spot of child-bed taint,
    Purification in the old Law did save,
    And such, as yet once more I trust to have
    Full sight of her in Heaven without restraint,
Came vested all in white, pure as her mind:
    Her face was vail'd, yet to my fancied sight,
    Love, sweetness, goodness, in her person shin'd
So clear, as in no face with more delight.
    But O as to embrace me she enclin'd
    I wak'd, she fled, and day brought back my night.

322. *Light*

HAIL holy light, ofspring of Heav'n first-born,
    Or of th' Eternal Coeternal beam
May I express thee unblam'd? since God is light,
And never but in unapproachéd light
Dwelt from Eternitie, dwelt then in thee,
Bright effluence of bright essence increate.
Or hear'st thou rather pure Ethereal stream,
Whose Fountain who shall tell? before the Sun,
Before the Heavens thou wert, and at the voice
Of God, as with a Mantle didst invest
The rising world of waters dark and deep,
Won from the void and formless infinite.
Thee I re-visit now with bolder wing,
Escap't the Stygian Pool, though long detain'd
In that obscure sojourn, while in my flight
Through utter and through middle darkness borne
With other notes then to th' Orphean Lyre

I sung of Chaos and Eternal Night,
Taught by the heav'nly Muse to venture down
The dark descent, and up to reascend,
Though hard and rare: thee I revisit safe,
And feel thy sovran vital Lamp; but thou
Revisit'st not these eyes, that rowle in vain
To find thy piercing ray, and find no dawn;
So thick a drop serene hath quencht thir Orbs,
Or dim suffusion veil'd. Yet not the more
Cease I to wander where the Muses haunt
Cleer Spring, or shadie Grove, or Sunnie Hill,
Smit with the love of sacred song; but chief
Thee *Sion* and the flowrie Brooks beneath
That wash thy hallowd feet, and warbling flow,
Nightly I visit: nor somtimes forget
Those other two equal'd with me in Fate,
So were I equal'd with them in renown.
Blind Thamyris and blind Mæonides,
And Tiresias and Phineus Prophets old.
Then feed on thoughts, that voluntarie move
Harmonious numbers; as the wakeful Bird
Sings darkling, and in shadiest Covert hid
Tunes her nocturnal Note. Thus with the Year
Seasons return, but not to me returns
Day, or the sweet approach of Ev'n or Morn,
Or sight of vernal bloom, or Summers Rose,
Or flocks, or herds, or human face divine;
But cloud in stead, and ever-during dark
Surrounds me, from the chearful waies of men
Cut off, and for the Book of knowledg fair
Presented with a Universal blanc
Of Natures works to mee expung'd and ras'd,
And wisdome at one entrance quite shut out.
So much the rather thou Celestial light
Shine inward, and the mind through all her powers
Irradiate, there plant eyes, all mist from thence

Purge and disperse, that I may see and tell
Of things invisible to mortal sight.

From 'Samson Agonistes'

323.   *i*

OH how comely it is and how reviving
   To the Spirits of just men long opprest!
When God into the hands of thir deliverer
Puts invincible might
To quell the mighty of the Earth, th' oppressour,
The brute and boist'rous force of violent men
Hardy and industrious to support
Tyrannic power, but raging to pursue
The righteous and all such as honour Truth;
He all thir Ammunition
And feats of War defeats
With plain Heroic magnitude of mind
And celestial vigour arm'd,
Thir Armories and Magazins contemns,
Renders them useless, while
With wingéd expedition
Swift as the lightning glance he executes
His errand on the wicked, who surpris'd
Lose thir defence distracted and amaz'd.

324.   *ii*

ALL is best, though we oft doubt,
   What th' unsearchable dispose
Of highest wisdom brings about,
And ever best found in the close.
Oft he seems to hide his face,
But unexpectedly returns
And to his faithful Champion hath in place

Bore witness gloriously; whence Gaza mourns
And all that band them to resist
His uncontroulable intent.
His servants he with new acquist
Of true experience from this great event
With peace and consolation hath dismist,
And calm of mind all passion spent.

SIR JOHN SUCKLING

1609–1642

325.   *A Doubt of Martyrdom*

O FOR some honest lover's ghost,
   Some kind unbodied post
   Sent from the shades below!
   I strangely long to know
Whether the noble chaplets wear
Those that their mistress' scorn did bear
   Or those that were used kindly.

For whatsoe'er they tell us here
   To make those sufferings dear,
      'Twill there, I fear, be found
      That to the being crown'd
T' have loved alone will not suffice,
Unless we also have been wise
   And have our loves enjoy'd.

What posture can we think him in
   That, here unloved, again
      Departs, and 's thither gone
      Where each sits by his own?
Or how can that Elysium be
Where I my mistress still must see
   Circled in other's arms?

For there the judges all are just,
And Sophonisba must
Be his whom she held dear,
Not his who loved her here.
The sweet Philoclea, since she died,
Lies by her Pirocles his side,
Not by Amphialus.

Some bays, perchance, or myrtle bough
For difference crowns the brow
Of those kind souls that were
The noble martyrs here:
And if that be the only odds
(As who can tell?), ye kinder gods,
Give me the woman here!

326.   *The Constant Lover*

OUT upon it, I have loved
Three whole days together!
And am like to love three more,
If it prove fair weather.

Time shall moult away his wings
Ere he shall discover
In the whole wide world again
Such a constant lover.

But the spite on 't is, no praise
Is due at all to me:
Love with me had made no stays,
Had it any been but she.

Had it any been but she,
And that very face,
There had been at least ere this
A dozen dozen in her place.

35

327. *Why So Pale and Wan?*

WHY so pale and wan, fond lover?
    Prithee, why so pale?
Will, when looking well can't move her,
    Looking ill prevail?
    Prithee, why so pale?

Why so dull and mute, young sinner?
    Prithee, why so mute?
Will, when speaking well can't win her,
    Saying nothing do 't?
    Prithee, why so mute?

Quit, quit for shame! This will not move;
    This cannot take her.
If of herself she will not love,
    Nothing can make her:
    The devil take her!

328. *When, Dearest, I But Think of Thee*

WHEN, dearest, I but think of thee,
    Methinks all things that lovely be
        Are present, and my soul delighted:
For beauties that from worth arise
Are like the grace of deities,
        Still present with us, tho' unsighted.

Thus while I sit and sigh the day
With all his borrow'd lights away,
        Till night's black wings do overtake me,
Thinking on thee, thy beauties then,
As sudden lights do sleepy men,
        So they by their bright rays awake me.

Thus absence dies, and dying proves
No absence can subsist with loves
    That do partake of fair perfection:
Since in the darkest night they may
By love's quick motion find a way
    To see each other by reflection.

The waving sea can with each flood
Bathe some high promont that hath stood
    Far from the main up in the river:
O think not then but love can do
As much! for that's an ocean too,
    Which flows not every day, but ever!

SIR RICHARD FANSHAWE

1608–1666

329.   *A Rose*

BLOWN in the morning, thou shalt fade ere noon.
   What boots a life which in such haste forsakes thee?
Thou'rt wondrous frolic, being to die so soon,
And passing proud a little colour makes thee.
If thee thy brittle beauty so deceives,
Know then the thing that swells thee is thy bane;
For the same beauty doth, in bloody leaves,
The sentence of thy early death contain.
Some clown's coarse lungs will poison thy sweet flower,
If by the careless plough thou shalt be torn;
And many Herods lie in wait each hour
To murder thee as soon as thou art born—
    Nay, force thy bud to blow—their tyrant breath
    Anticipating life, to hasten death!

WILLIAM CARTWRIGHT

1611–1643

330.   *To Chloe*

Who for His Sake Wished Herself Younger

THERE are two births; the one when light
First strikes the new awaken'd sense;
The other when two souls unite,
    And we must count our life from thence:
When you loved me and I loved you
Then both of us were born anew.

Love then to us new souls did give
    And in those souls did plant new powers;
Since when another life we live,
    The breath we breathe is his, not ours:
Love makes those young whom age doth chill,
And whom he finds young keeps young still.

331.   *Falsehood*

STILL do the stars impart their light
To those that travel in the night;
Still time runs on, nor doth the hand
Or shadow on the dial stand;
The streams still glide and constant are:
        Only thy mind
        Untrue I find,
        Which carelessly
        Neglects to be
Like stream or shadow, hand or star.

Fool that I am! I do recall
My words, and swear thou'rt like them all,
Thou seem'st like stars to nourish fire,

38

But O how cold is thy desire!
And like the hand upon the brass
     Thou point'st at me
     In mockery;
     If I come nigh
     Shade-like thou'lt fly,
And as the stream with murmur pass.

332.   *On the Queen's Return*
from the Low Countries

HALLOW the threshold, crown the posts anew!
    The day shall have its due.
Twist all our victories into one bright wreath,
    On which let honour breathe;
Then throw it round the temples of our Queen!
'Tis she that must preserve those glories green.

When greater tempests than on sea before
    Received her on the shore;
When she was shot at 'for the King's own good'
    By legions hired to blood;
How bravely did she do, how bravely bear!
And show'd, though they durst rage, she durst not fear.

Courage was cast about her like a dress
    Of solemn comeliness:
A gather'd mind and an untroubled face
    Did give her dangers grace:
Thus, arm'd with innocence, secure they move
Whose highest 'treason' is but highest love.

333. *On a Virtuous Young Gentlewoman That Died Suddenly*

SHE who to Heaven more Heaven doth annex,
  Whose lowest thought was above all our sex,
Accounted nothing death but t' be repriev'd,
And died as free from sickness as she lived.
Others are dragg'd away, or must be driven,
She only saw her time and stept to Heaven;
Where seraphims view all her glories o'er,
As one return'd that had been there before.
For while she did this lower world adorn,
Her body seem'd rather assumed than born;
So rarified, advanced, so pure and whole,
That body might have been another's soul;
And equally a miracle it were
That she could die, or that she could live here.

JAMES GRAHAM, MARQUIS OF MONTROSE

1612–1650

334. *I'll Never Love Thee More*

MY dear and only Love, I pray
    That little world of thee
Be govern'd by no other sway
    Than purest monarchy;
For if confusion have a part
    (Which virtuous souls abhor),
And hold a synod in thine heart,
    I'll never love thee more.

Like Alexander I will reign,
    And I will reign alone;
My thoughts did evermore disdain
    A rival on my throne.

He either fears his fate too much,
 Or his deserts are small,
That dares not put it to the touch,
 To gain or lose it all.

And in the empire of thine heart,
 Where I should solely be,
If others do pretend a part
 Or dare to vie with me,
Or if *Committees* thou erect,
 And go on such a score,
I'll laugh and sing at thy neglect,
 And never love thee more.

But if thou wilt prove faithful then,
 And constant of thy word,
I'll make thee glorious by my pen
 And famous by my sword;
I'll serve thee in such noble ways
 Was never heard before;
I'll crown and deck thee all with bays,
 And love thee more and more.

THOMAS JORDAN

1612?–1685

335. *Coronemus Nos Rosis*
Antequam Marcescant

LET us drink and be merry, dance, joke, and rejoice,
 With claret and sherry, theorbo and voice!
The changeable world to our joy is unjust,
 All treasure's uncertain,
 Then down with your dust!
In frolics dispose your pounds, shillings, and pence,
For we shall be nothing a hundred years hence.

We'll sport and be free with Moll, Betty, and Dolly,
Have oysters and lobsters to cure melancholy:
Fish-dinners will make a man spring like a flea,
      Dame Venus, love's lady,
      Was born of the sea;
With her and with Bacchus we'll tickle the sense,
For we shall be past it a hundred years hence.

Your most beautiful bride who with garlands is crown'd
And kills with each glance as she treads on the ground,
Whose lightness and brightness doth shine in such splendour
      That none but the stars
      Are thought fit to attend her,
Though now she be pleasant and sweet to the sense,
Will be damnable mouldy a hundred years hence.

Then why should we turmoil in cares and in fears,
Turn all our tranquill'ty to sighs and to tears?
Let's eat, drink, and play till the worms do corrupt us,
      'Tis certain, *Post mortem*
      Nulla voluptas.
For health, wealth and beauty, wit, learning and sense,
Must all come to nothing a hundred years hence.

RICHARD CRASHAW

1613?–1649

336. *Wishes to His Supposed Mistress*

W HOE'ER she be—
    That not impossible She
That shall command my heart and me:

Where'er she lie,
    Lock'd up from mortal eye
    In shady leaves of destiny:

Till that ripe birth
Of studied Fate stand forth,
And teach her fair steps to our earth:

Till that divine
Idea take a shrine
Of crystal flesh, through which to shine:

Meet you her, my Wishes,
Bespeak her to my blisses,
And be ye call'd my absent kisses.

I wish her Beauty,
That owes not all its duty
To gaudy tire, or glist'ring shoe-tie:

Something more than
Taffata or tissue can,
Or rampant feather, or rich fan.

A Face, that's best
By its own beauty drest,
And can alone commend the rest.

A Face, made up
Out of no other shop
Than what Nature's white hand sets ope.

A Cheek, where youth
And blood, with pen of truth,
Write what the reader sweetly ru'th.

A Cheek, where grows
More than a morning rose,
Which to no box his being owes.

Lips, where all day
A lover's kiss may play,
Yet carry nothing thence away.

Looks, that oppress
Their richest tires, but dress
And clothe their simplest nakedness.

Eyes, that displace
The neighbour diamond, and outface
That sunshine by their own sweet grace.

Tresses, that wear
Jewels but to declare
How much themselves more precious are:

Whose native ray
Can tame the wanton day
Of gems that in their bright shades play.

Each ruby there,
Or pearl that dare appear,
Be its own blush, be its own tear.

A well-tamed Heart,
For whose more noble smart
Love may be long choosing a dart.

Eyes, that bestow
Full quivers on love's bow,
Yet pay less arrows than they owe.

Smiles, that can warm
The blood, yet teach a charm,
That chastity shall take no harm.

Blushes, that bin
The burnish of no sin,
Nor flames of aught too hot within.

Joys, that confess
Virtue their mistress,
And have no other head to dress.

Fears, fond and slight
As the coy bride's, when night
First does the longing lover right.

Days, that need borrow
No part of their good-morrow
From a fore-spent night of sorrow.

Days, that in spite
Of darkness, by the light
Of a clear mind, are day all night.

Nights, sweet as they,
Made short by lovers' play,
Yet long by th' absence of the day.

Life, that dares send
A challenge to his end,
And when it comes, say, 'Welcome, friend!'

Sydneian showers
Of sweet discourse, whose powers
Can crown old Winter's head with flowers.

Soft silken hours,
Open suns, shady bowers;
'Bove all, nothing within that lowers.

Whate'er delight
Can make Day's forehead bright,
Or give down to the wings of Night.

I wish her store
Of worth may leave her poor
Of wishes; and I wish—no more.

Now, if Time knows
That Her, whose radiant brows
Weave them a garland of my vows;

Her, whose just bays
My future hopes can raise,
A trophy to her present praise;

Her, that dares be
What these lines wish to see;
I seek no further, it is She.

'Tis She, and here,
Lo! I unclothe and clear
My Wishes' cloudy character.

May she enjoy it
Whose merit dare apply it,
But modesty dares still deny it!

Such worth as this is
Shall fix my flying Wishes,
And determine them to kisses.

Let her full glory,
My fancies, fly before ye;
Be ye my fictions—but her story.

337.   *The Weeper*

HAIL, sister springs,
        Parents of silver-footed rills!
Ever bubbling things,
Thawing crystal, snowy hills!
        Still spending, never spent; I mean
        Thy fair eyes, sweet Magdalene.

Heavens thy fair eyes be;
Heavens of ever-falling stars;
    'Tis seed-time still with thee,
And stars thou sow'st whose harvest dares
        Promise the earth to countershine
        Whatever makes Heaven's forehead fine.

Every morn from hence
A brisk cherub something sips
　Whose soft influence
Adds sweetness to his sweetest lips;
　　Then to his music: and his song
　　Tastes of this breakfast all day long.

　When some new bright guest
Takes up among the stars a room,
　And Heaven will make a feast,
Angels with their bottles come,
　　And draw from these full eyes of thine
　　Their Master's water, their own wine.

The dew no more will weep
The primrose's pale cheek to deck;
　The dew no more will sleep
Nuzzled in the lily's neck:
　　Much rather would it tremble here,
　　And leave them both to be thy tear.

　When sorrow would be seen
In her brightest majesty,
　—For she is a Queen—
Then is she drest by none but thee:
　　Then and only then she wears
　　Her richest pearls—I mean thy tears.

　Not in the evening's eyes,
When they red with weeping are
　For the Sun that dies,
Sits Sorrow with a face so fair.
　　Nowhere but here did ever meet
　　Sweetness so sad, sadness so sweet.

　Does the night arise?
Still thy tears do fall and fall.
　Does night lose her eyes?
Still the fountain weeps for all.

47

Let day and night do what they will,
Thou hast thy task, thou weepest still.

Not *So long she lived*
Will thy tomb report of thee;
But *So long she grieved*:
Thus must we date thy memory.
Others by days, by months, by years,
Measure their ages, thou by tears.

Say, ye bright brothers,
The fugitive sons of those fair eyes
Your fruitful mothers,
What make you here? What hopes can 'tice
You to be born? What cause can borrow
You from those nests of noble sorrow?

Whither away so fast?
For sure the sordid earth
Your sweetness cannot taste,
Nor does the dust deserve your birth.
Sweet, whither haste you then? O say,
Why you trip so fast away?

We go not to seek
The darlings of Aurora's bed,
The rose's modest cheek,
Nor the violet's humble head.
No such thing: we go to meet
A worthier object—our Lord's feet.

338. A Hymn to the Name and Honour of the Admirable Saint Teresa

LOVE, thou are absolute, sole Lord
Of life and death. To prove the word,
We'll now appeal to none of all
Those thy old soldiers, great and tall,

Ripe men of martyrdom, that could reach down
With strong arms their triumphant crown:
Such as could with lusty breath
Speak loud, unto the face of death,
Their great Lord's glorious name; to none
Of those whose spacious bosoms spread a throne
For love at large to fill. Spare blood and sweat:
We'll see Him take a private seat,
And make His mansion in the mild
And milky soul of a soft child.

Scarce has she learnt to lisp a name
Of martyr, yet she thinks it shame
Life should so long play with that breath
Which spent can buy so brave a death.
She never undertook to know
What death with love should have to do.
Nor has she e'er yet understood
Why, to show love, she should shed blood;
Yet, though she cannot tell you why,
She can love, and she can die.
Scarce has she blood enough to make
A guilty sword blush for her sake;
Yet has a heart dares hope to prove
How much less strong is death than love . . . .

Since 'tis not to be had at home,
She'll travel for a martyrdom.
No home for her, confesses she,
But where she may a martyr be.
She'll to the Moors, and trade with them
For this unvalued diadem;
She offers them her dearest breath,
With Christ's name in 't, in change for death:
She'll bargain with them, and will give
Them God, and teach them how to live
In Him; or, if they this deny,

For Him she'll teach them how to die.
So shall she leave amongst them sown
Her Lord's blood, or at least her own.

Farewell then, all the world, adieu!
Teresa is no more for you.
Farewell all pleasures, sports, and joys,
Never till now esteeméd toys!

Farewell whatever dear may be—
Mother's arms, or father's knee!
Farewell house, and farewell home!
She's for the Moors and Martyrdom.

Sweet, not so fast; lo! thy fair spouse,
Whom thou seek'st with so swift vows,
Calls thee back, and bids thee come
T' embrace a milder martyrdom . . . .

O how oft shalt thou complain
Of a sweet and subtle pain!
Of intolerable joys!
Of a death, in which who dies
Loves his death, and dies again,
And would for ever so be slain;
And lives and dies, and knows not why
To live, but that he still may die!
How kindly will thy gentle heart
Kiss the sweetly-killing dart!
And close in his embraces keep
Those delicious wounds, that weep
Balsam, to heal themselves with thus,
When these thy deaths, so numerous,
Shall all at once die into one,
And melt thy soul's sweet mansion;
Like a soft lump of incense, hasted
By too hot a fire, and wasted
Into perfuming clouds, so fast

Shalt thou exhale to heaven at last
In a resolving sigh, and then,—
O what? Ask not the tongues of men.

Angels cannot tell; suffice,
Thyself shalt feel thine own full joys,
And hold them fast for ever there.
So soon as thou shalt first appear,
The moon of maiden stars, thy white
Mistress, attended by such bright
Souls as thy shining self, shall come,
And in her first ranks make thee room;
Where, 'mongst her snowy family,
Immortal welcomes wait for thee.
O what delight, when she shall stand
And teach thy lips heaven, with her hand,
On which thou now may'st to thy wishes
Heap up thy consecrated kisses!
What joy shall seize thy soul, when she,
Bending her bless̀ed eyes on thee,
Those second smiles of heaven, shall dart
Her mild rays through thy melting heart!

Angels, thy old friends, there shall greet thee,
Glad at their own home now to meet thee.
All thy good works which went before,
And waited for thee at the door,
Shall own thee there; and all in one
Weave a constellation
Of crowns, with which the King, thy spouse,
Shall build up thy triumphant brows.
All thy old woes shall now smile on thee,
And thy pains sit bright upon thee:
All thy sorrows here shall shine,
And thy sufferings be divine.
Tears shall take comfort, and turn gems,
And wrongs repent to diadems.

Even thy deaths shall live, and new
Dress the soul which late they slew.
Thy wounds shall blush to such bright scars
As keep account of the Lamb's wars.

Those rare works, where thou shalt leave writ
Love's noble history, with wit
Taught thee by none but Him, while here
They feed our souls, shall clothe thine there.
Each heavenly word by whose hid flame
Our hard hearts shall strike fire, the same
Shall flourish on thy brows, and be
Both fire to us and flame to thee;
Whose light shall live bright in thy face
By glory, in our hearts by grace.
Thou shalt look round about, and see
Thousands of crown'd souls throng to be
Themselves thy crown, sons of thy vows,
The virgin-births with which thy spouse
Made fruitful thy fair soul; go now,
And with them all about thee bow
To Him; put on, He'll say, put on,
My rosy Love, that thy rich zone,
Sparkling with the sacred flames
Of thousand souls, whose happy names
Heaven keeps upon thy score: thy bright
Life brought them first to kiss the light
That kindled them to stars; and so
Thou with the Lamb, thy Lord, shalt go.
And, wheresoe'er He sets His white
Steps, walk with Him those ways of light,
Which who in death would live to see,
Must learn in life to die like thee.

339.   *Upon the Book and Picture of the Seraphical Saint Teresa*

O THOU undaunted daughter of desires!
　　By all thy dower of lights and fires;
By all the eagle in thee, all the dove;
By all thy lives and deaths of love;
By thy large draughts of intellectual day,
And by thy thirsts of love more large than they;
By all thy brim-fill'd bowls of fierce desire,
By thy last morning's draught of liquid fire;
By the full kingdom of that final kiss
That seized thy parting soul, and seal'd thee His;
By all the Heav'n thou hast in Him
(Fair sister of the seraphim!);
By all of Him we have in thee;
Leave nothing of myself in me.
Let me so read thy life, that I
Unto all life of mine may die!

340.   *Verses from the Shepherds' Hymn*

WE saw Thee in Thy balmy nest,
　　Young dawn of our eternal day;
We saw Thine eyes break from the East,
　　And chase the trembling shades away:
We saw Thee, and we blest the sight,
We saw Thee by Thine own sweet light.

Poor world, said I, what wilt thou do
　　To entertain this starry stranger?
Is this the best thou canst bestow—
　　A cold and not too cleanly manger?
Contend, the powers of heaven and earth,
To fit a bed for this huge birth.

Proud world, said I, cease your contest,
  And let the mighty babe alone;
The phœnix builds the phœnix' nest,
  Love's architecture is His own.
The babe, whose birth embraves this morn,
Made His own bed ere He was born.

I saw the curl'd drops, soft and slow,
  Come hovering o'er the place's head,
Off'ring their whitest sheets of snow,
  To furnish the fair infant's bed.
Forbear, said I, be not too bold;
Your fleece is white, but 'tis too cold.

I saw th' obsequious seraphim
  Their rosy fleece of fire bestow,
For well they now can spare their wings,
  Since Heaven itself lies here below.
Well done, said I; but are you sure
Your down, so warm, will pass for pure?

No, no, your King's not yet to seek
  Where to repose His royal head;
See, see how soon His new-bloom'd cheek
  'Twixt mother's breasts is gone to bed!
Sweet choice, said we; no way but so,
Not to lie cold, you sleep in snow!

She sings Thy tears asleep, and dips
  Her kisses in Thy weeping eye;
She spreads the red leaves of Thy lips,
  That in their buds yet blushing lie.
She 'gainst those mother diamonds tries
The points of her young eagle's eyes.

Welcome—tho' not to those gay flies,
  Gilded i' th' beams of earthly kings,
Slippery souls in smiling eyes—

But to poor shepherds, homespun things,
Whose wealth 's their flocks, whose wit 's to be
Well read in their simplicity.

Yet, when young April's husband show'rs
    Shall bless the fruitful Maia's bed,
We'll bring the first-born of her flowers,
    To kiss Thy feet and crown Thy head.
To Thee, dread Lamb! whose love must keep
The shepherds while they feed their sheep.

To Thee, meek Majesty, soft King
    Of simple graces and sweet loves!
Each of us his lamb will bring,
    Each his pair of silver doves!
At last, in fire of Thy fair eyes,
Ourselves become our own best sacrifice!

341. *Christ Crucified*

THY restless feet now cannot go
    For us and our eternal good,
As they were ever wont. What though
    They swim, alas! in their own flood?

Thy hands to give Thou canst not lift,
    Yet will Thy hand still giving be;
It gives, but O, itself's the gift!
    It gives tho' bound, tho' bound 'tis free!

342. *An Epitaph upon Husband and Wife*

Who Died and Were Buried Together

TO these whom death again did wed
    This grave's the second marriage-bed.

For though the hand of Fate could force
'Twixt soul and body a divorce,
It could not sever man and wife,
Because they both lived but one life.
Peace, good reader, do not weep;
Peace, the lovers are asleep.
They, sweet turtles, folded lie
In the last knot that love could tie.
Let them sleep, let them sleep on,
Till the stormy night be gone,
And the eternal morrow dawn;
Then the curtains will be drawn,
And they wake into a light
Whose day shall never die in night.

RICHARD LOVELACE

1618–1658

343. *To Lucasta, Going to the Wars*

TELL me not, Sweet, I am unkind,
    That from the nunnery
Of thy chaste breast and quiet mind
    To war and arms I fly.

True, a new mistress now I chase,
    The first foe in the field;
And with a stronger faith embrace
    A sword, a horse, a shield.

Yet this inconstancy is such
    As thou too shalt adore;
I could not love thee, Dear, so much,
    Loved I not Honour more.

344. *To Lucasta, Going beyond the Seas*

IF to be absent were to be
    Away from thee;
  Or that when I am gone
  You or I were alone;
Then, my Lucasta, might I crave
Pity from blustering wind or swallowing wave.

  But I'll not sigh one blast or gale
    To swell my sail,
  Or pay a tear to 'suage
  The foaming blue god's rage;
For whether he will let me pass
Or no, I'm still as happy as I was.

  Though seas and land betwixt us both,
    Our faith and troth,
  Like separated souls,
  All time and space controls:
Above the highest sphere we meet
Unseen, unknown; and greet as Angels greet.

  So then we do anticipate
    Our after-fate,
  And are alive i' the skies,
  If thus our lips and eyes
Can speak like spirits unconfined
In Heaven, their earthy bodies left behind.

345.   *Gratiana Dancing*

SHE beat the happy pavément—
  By such a star made firmament,
  Which now no more the roof envíes!
    But swells up high, with Atlas even,
    Bearing the brighter nobler heaven,
  And, in her, all the deities.

Each step trod out a Lover's thought,
And the ambitious hopes he brought
Chain'd to her brave feet with such arts,
Such sweet command and gentle awe,
As, when she ceased, we sighing saw
The floor lay paved with broken hearts.

346.   *To Amarantha, That She Would Dishevel Her Hair*

AMARANTHA sweet and fair,
Ah, braid no more that shining hair!
As my curious hand or eye
Hovering round thee, let it fly!

Let it fly as unconfined
As its calm ravisher the wind,
Who hath left his darling, th' East,
To wanton o'er that spicy nest.

Every tress must be confest,
But neatly tangled at the best;
Like a clew of golden thread
Most excellently ravellèd.

Do not then wind up that light
In ribbands, and o'ercloud in night,
Like the Sun in 's early ray;
But shake your head, and scatter day!

347.   *The Grasshopper*

O THOU that swing'st upon the waving hair
Of some well-fillèd oaten beard,
Drunk every night with a delicious tear
Dropt thee from heaven, where thou wert rear'd!

The joys of earth and air are thine entire,
    That with thy feet and wings dost hop and fly;
And when thy poppy works, thou dost retire
    To thy carved acorn-bed to lie.

Up with the day, the Sun thou welcom'st then,
    Sport'st in the gilt plaits of his beams,
And all these merry days mak'st merry men,
    Thyself, and melancholy streams.

348.   *To Althea, from Prison*

WHEN Love with unconfinéd wings
    Hovers within my gates,
And my divine Althea brings
    To whisper at the grates;
When I lie tangled in her hair
    And fetter'd to her eye,
The birds that wanton in the air
    Know no such liberty.

When flowing cups run swiftly round
    With no allaying Thames,
Our careless heads with roses bound,
    Our hearts with loyal flames;
When thirsty grief in wine we steep,
    When healths and draughts go free—
Fishes that tipple in the deep
    Know no such liberty.

When, like committed linnets, I
    With shriller throat shall sing
The sweetness, mercy, majesty,
    And glories of my King;
When I shall voice aloud how good
    He is, how great should be,
Enlargéd winds, that curl the flood,
    Know no such liberty.

Stone walls do not a prison make,
    Nor iron bars a cage;
Minds innocent and quiet take
    That for an hermitage;
If I have freedom in my love
    And in my soul am free,
Angels alone, that soar above,
    Enjoy such liberty.

ABRAHAM COWLEY

1618–1667

Anacreontics

349.   ### *1. Drinking*

THE thirsty earth soaks up the rain,
    And drinks and gapes for drink again;
The plants suck in the earth, and are
With constant drinking fresh and fair;
The sea itself (which one would think
Should have but little need of drink)
Drinks twice ten thousand rivers up,
So fill'd that they o'erflow the cup.
The busy Sun (and one would guess
By 's drunken fiery face no less)
Drinks up the sea, and when he 's done,
The Moon and Stars drink up the Sun:
They drink and dance by their own light,
They drink and revel all the night:
Nothing in Nature's sober found,
But an eternal health goes round.
Fill up the bowl, then, fill it high,
Fill all the glasses there—for why
Should every creature drink but I?
Why, man of morals, tell me why?

350. ## 2. The Epicure

UNDERNEATH this myrtle shade,
On flowery beds supinely laid,
With odorous oils my head o'erflowing,
And around it roses growing,
What should I do but drink away
The heat and troubles of the day?
In this more than kingly state
Love himself on me shall wait.
Fill to me, Love! nay, fill it up!
And mingled cast into the cup
Wit and mirth and noble fires,
Vigorous health and gay desires.
The wheel of life no less will stay
In a smooth than rugged way:
Since it equally doth flee,
Let the motion pleasant be.
Why do we precious ointments shower?—
Nobler wines why do we pour?—
Beauteous flowers why do we spread
Upon the monuments of the dead?
Nothing they but dust can show,
Or bones that hasten to be so.
Crown me with roses while I live,
Now your wines and ointments give:
After death I nothing crave,
Let me alive my pleasures have:
All are Stoics in the grave.

351. ## 3. The Swallow

FOOLISH prater, what dost thou
So early at my window do?
Cruel bird, thou'st ta'en away
A dream out of my arms to-day;
A dream that ne'er must equall'd be

61

By all that waking eyes may see.
Thou this damage to repair
Nothing half so sweet and fair,
Nothing half so good, canst bring,
Tho' men say thou bring'st the Spring.

352. *On the Death of Mr. William Hervey*

IT was a dismal and a fearful night:
  Scarce could the Morn drive on th' unwilling Light,
When Sleep, Death's image, left my troubled breast
    By something liker Death possest.
My eyes with tears did uncommanded flow,
    And on my soul hung the dull weight
    Of some intolerable fate.
What bell was that? Ah me! too much I know!

My sweet companion and my gentle peer,
Why hast thou left me thus unkindly here,
Thy end for ever and my life to moan?
    O, thou hast left me all alone!
Thy soul and body, when death's agony
    Besieged around thy noble heart,
    Did not with more reluctance part
Than I, my dearest Friend, do part from thee.

My dearest Friend, would I had died for thee!
Life and this world henceforth will tedious be:
Nor shall I know hereafter what to do
    If once my griefs prove tedious too.
Silent and sad I walk about all day,
    As sullen ghosts stalk speechless by
    Where their hid treasures lie;
Alas! my treasure's gone; why do I stay?

Say, for you saw us, ye immortal lights,
How oft unwearied have we spent the nights,

Till the Ledæan stars, so famed for love,
    Wonder'd at us from above!
We spent them not in toys, in lusts, or wine;
    But search of deep Philosophy,
    Wit, Eloquence, and Poetry—
Arts which I loved, for they, my Friend, were thine.

Ye fields of Cambridge, our dear Cambridge, say
Have ye not seen us walking every day?
Was there a tree about which did not know
    The love betwixt us two?
    Henceforth, ye gentle trees, for ever fade;
Or your sad branches thicker join
    And into darksome shades combine,
Dark as the grave wherein my Friend is laid!

Large was his soul: as large a soul as e'er
Submitted to inform a body here;
High as the place 'twas shortly in Heaven to have,
    But low and humble as his grave.
So high that all the virtues there did come,
    As to their chiefest seat
    Conspicuous and great;
So low, that for me too it made a room.

Knowledge he only sought, and so soon caught
As if for him Knowledge had rather sought;
Nor did more learning ever crowded lie
    In such a short mortality.
Whene'er the skilful youth discoursed or writ,
    Still did the notions throng
    About his eloquent tongue;
Nor could his ink flow faster than his wit.

His mirth was the pure spirits of various wit,
Yet never did his God or friends forget;
And when deep talk and wisdom came in view,
    Retired, and gave to them their due.

For the rich help of books he always took,
    Though his own searching mind before
    Was so with notions written o'er,
As if wise Nature had made that her book.

With as much zeal, devotion, piety,
He always lived, as other saints do die.
Still with his soul severe account he kept,
    Weeping all debts out ere he slept.
Then down in peace and innocence he lay,
    Like the Sun's laborious light,
    Which still in water sets at night,
Unsullied with his journey of the day.

But happy Thou, ta'en from this frantic age,
Where ignorance and hypocrisy does rage!
A fitter time for Heaven no soul e'er chose—
    The place now only free from those.
There 'mong the blest thou dost for ever shine;
    And wheresoe'er thou casts thy view
    Upon that white and radiant crew,
See'st not a soul clothed with more light than thine.

353. *The Wish*

WELL then! I now do plainly see
    This busy world and I shall ne'er agree.
The very honey of all earthly joy
Does of all meats the soonest cloy;
    And they, methinks, deserve my pity
Who for it can endure the stings,
The crowd and buzz and murmurings,
    Of this great hive, the city.

Ah, yet, ere I descend to the grave
May I a small house and large garden have;
And a few friends, and many books, both true,
Both wise, and both delightful too!

And since love ne'er will from me flee,
A Mistress moderately fair,
And good as guardian angels are,
    Only beloved and loving me.

O fountains! when in you shall I
Myself eased of unpeaceful thoughts espy?
O fields! O woods! when, when shall I be made
Thy happy tenant of your shade?
    Here's the spring-head of Pleasure's flood:
Here 's wealthy Nature's treasury,
Where all the riches lie that she
    Has coin'd and stamp'd for good.

Pride and ambition here
Only in far-fetch'd metaphors appear;
Here nought but winds can hurtful murmurs scatter,
And nought but Echo flatter.
    The gods, when they descended, hither
From heaven did always choose their way:
And therefore we may boldly say
    That 'tis the way too thither.

How happy here should I
And one dear She live, and embracing die!
She who is all the world, and can exclude
In deserts solitude.
    I should have then this only fear:
Lest men, when they my pleasures see,
Should hither throng to live like me,
    And so make a city here.

ALEXANDER BROME

1620–1666

354.   *The Resolve*

TELL me not of a face that 's fair,
    Nor lip and cheek that 's red,
Nor of the tresses of her hair,
    Nor curls in order laid,
Nor of a rare seraphic voice
    That like an angel sings;
Though if I were to take my choice
    I would have all these things:
But if that thou wilt have me love,
    And it must be a she,
The only argument can move
    Is that she will love me.

The glories of your ladies be
    But metaphors of things,
And but resemble what we see
    Each common object brings.
Roses out-red their lips and cheeks,
    Lilies their whiteness stain;
What fool is he that shadows seeks
    And may the substance gain?
Then if thou'lt have me love a lass,
    Let it be one that's kind:
Else I'm a servant to the glass
    That 's with Canary lined.

ANDREW MARVELL

1621–1678

355. *An Horatian Ode*

Upon Cromwell's Return from Ireland

THE forward youth that would appear
Must now forsake his Muses dear,
 Nor in the shadows sing
 His numbers languishing.

'Tis time to leave the books in dust,
And oil the unused armour's rust,
 Removing from the wall
 The corslet of the hall.

So restless Cromwell could not cease
In the inglorious arts of peace,
 But through adventurous war
 Urgéd his active star:

And like the three-fork'd lightning, first
Breaking the clouds where it was nurst,
 Did thorough his own side
 His fiery way divide:

For 'tis all one to courage high,
The emulous, or enemy;
 And with such, to enclose
 Is more than to oppose.

Then burning through the air he went
And palaces and temples rent;
 And Cæsar's head at last
 Did through his laurels blast.

'Tis madness to resist or blame
The face of angry Heaven's flame;

And if we would speak true,
Much to the man is due,

Who, from his private gardens, where
He lived reservéd and austere
    (As if his highest plot
    To plant the bergamot),

Could by industrious valour climb
To ruin the great work of time,
    And cast the Kingdoms old
    Into another mould;

Though Justice against Fate complain,
And plead the ancient rights in vain—
    But those do hold or break
    As men are strong or weak—

Nature, that hateth emptiness,
Allows of penetration less,
    And therefore must make room
    Where greater spirits come.

What field of all the civil war
Where his were not the deepest scar?
    And Hampton shows what part
    He had of wiser art;

Where, twining subtle fears with hope,
He wove a net of such a scope
    That Charles himself might chase
    To Caresbrooke's narrow case;

That thence the Royal actor borne
The tragic scaffold might adorn:
    While round the arméd bands
    Did clap their bloody hands.

He nothing common did or mean
Upon that memorable scene,

> But with his keener eye
> The axe's edge did try;

Nor call'd the gods, with vulgar spite,
To vindicate his helpless right;
> But bow'd his comely head
> Down, as upon a bed.

This was that memorable hour
Which first assured the forcéd power:
> So when they did design
> The Capitol's first line,

A Bleeding Head, where they begun,
Did fright the architects to run;
> And yet in that the State
> Foresaw its happy fate!

And now the Irish are ashamed
To see themselves in one year tamed:
> So much one man can do
> That does both act and know.

They can affirm his praises best,
And have, though overcome, confest
> How good he is, how just
> And fit for highest trust.

Nor yet grown stiffer with command,
But still in the republic's hand—
> How fit he is to sway
> That can so well obey!

He to the Commons' feet presents
A Kingdom for his first year's rents,
> And, what he may, forbears
> His fame, to make it theirs:

And has his sword and spoils ungirt
To lay them at the public's skirt.

So when the falcon high
Falls heavy from the sky,

She, having kill'd, no more doth search
But on the next green bough to perch;
    Where, when he first does lure,
    The falconer has her sure.

What may not then our Isle presume
While victory his crest does plume?
    What may not others fear,
    If thus he crowns each year?

As Cæsar he, ere long, to Gaul,
To Italy an Hannibal,
    And to all States not free
    Shall climacteric be.

The Pict no shelter now shall find
Within his particolour'd mind,
    But, from this valour, sad
    Shrink underneath the plaid;

Happy, if in the tufted brake
The English hunter him mistake,
    Nor lay his hounds in near
    The Caledonian deer.

But thou, the war's and fortune's son,
March indefatigably on;
    And for the last effect,
    Still keep the sword erect:

Besides the force it has to fright
The spirits of the shady night,
    The same arts that did gain
    A power, must it maintain.

356. *A Garden*

Written after the Civil Wars

SEE how the flowers, as at parade,
　Under their colours stand display'd:
Each regiment in order grows,
That of the tulip, pink, and rose.
But when the vigilant patrol
Of stars walks round about the pole,
Their leaves, that to the stalks are curl'd,
Seem to their staves the ensigns furl'd.
Then in some flower's belovéd hut
Each bee, as sentinel, is shut,
And sleeps so too; but if once stirr'd,
She runs you through, nor asks the word.
O thou, that dear and happy Isle,
The garden of the world erewhile,
Thou Paradise of the four seas
Which Heaven planted us to please,
But, to exclude the world, did guard
With wat'ry if not flaming sword;
What luckless apple did we taste
To make us mortal and thee waste!
Unhappy! shall we never more
That sweet militia restore,
When gardens only had their towers,
And all the garrisons were flowers;
When roses only arms might bear,
And men did rosy garlands wear?

357. *To His Coy Mistress*

HAD we but world enough, and time,
This coyness, Lady, were no crime
We would sit down and think which way
To walk and pass our long love's day.
Thou by the Indian Ganges' side
Shouldst rubies find: I by the tide
Of Humber would complain. I would
Love you ten years before the Flood,
And you should, if you please, refuse
Till the conversion of the Jews.
My vegetable love should grow
Vaster than empires, and more slow;
An hundred years should go to praise
Thine eyes and on thy forehead gaze;
Two hundred to adore each breast,
But thirty thousand to the rest;
An age at least to every part,
And the last age should show your heart.
For, Lady, you deserve this state,
Nor would I love at lower rate.

But at my back I always hear
Time's wingéd chariot hurrying near;
And yonder all before us lie
Deserts of vast eternity.
Thy beauty shall no more be found,
Nor, in thy marble vault, shall sound
My echoing song: then worms shall try
That long preserved virginity,
And your quaint honour turn to dust,
And into ashes all my lust:
The grave 's a fine and private place,
But none, I think, do there embrace.

Now therefore, while the youthful hue
Sits on thy skin like morning dew,

And while thy willing soul transpires
At every pore with instant fires,
Now let us sport us while we may,
And now, like amorous birds of prey,
Rather at once our time devour
Than languish in his slow-chapt power.
Let us roll all our strength and all
Our sweetness up into one ball,
And tear our pleasures with rough strife
Thorough the iron gates of life:
Thus, though we cannot make our sun
Stand still, yet we will make him run.

358. *The Picture of Little T. C. in a Prospect of Flowers*

SEE with what simplicity
   This nymph begins her golden days!
In the green grass she loves to lie,
And there with her fair aspect tames
The wilder flowers, and gives them names;
   But only with the roses plays,
          And them does tell
What colour best becomes them, and what smell.

     Who can foretell for what high cause
     This darling of the gods was born?
     Yet this is she whose chaster laws
The wanton Love shall one day fear,
And, under her command severe,
     See his bow broke and ensigns torn.
          Happy who can
Appease this virtuous enemy of man!

slow-chapt] slow-jawed, slowly devouring.

73

O then let me in time compound
And parley with those conquering eyes,
  Ere they have tried their force to wound;
Ere with their glancing wheels they drive
In triumph over hearts that strive,
  And them that yield but more despise:
          Let me be laid,
Where I may see the glories from some shade.

  Meantime, whilst every verdant thing
Itself does at thy beauty charm,
  Reform the errors of the Spring;
Make that the tulips may have share
Of sweetness, seeing they are fair,
  And roses of their thorns disarm;
          But most procure
That violets may a longer age endure.

  But O, young beauty of the woods,
Whom Nature courts with fruits and flowers,
  Gather the flowers, but spare the buds;
Lest Flora, angry at thy crime
To kill her infants in their prime,
  Do quickly make th' example yours;
          And ere we see,
Nip in the blossom all our hopes and thee.

359.   *Thoughts in a Garden*

HOW vainly men themselves amaze
  To win the palm, the oak, or bays,
And their uncessant labours see
Crown'd from some single herb or tree,
Whose short and narrow-vergéd shade
Does prudently their toils upbraid;
While all the flowers and trees do close
To weave the garlands of repose!

Fair Quiet, have I found thee here,
And Innocence thy sister dear?
Mistaken long, I sought you then
In busy companies of men:
Your sacred plants, if here below,
Only among the plants will grow:
Society is all but rude
To this delicious solitude.

No white nor red was ever seen
So amorous as this lovely green.
Fond lovers, cruel as their flame,
Cut in these trees their mistress' name:
Little, alas! they know or heed
How far these beauties hers exceed!
Fair trees! wheres'e'er your barks I wound,
No name shall but your own be found.

When we have run our passions' heat,
Love hither makes his best retreat:
The gods, that mortal beauty chase,
Still in a tree did end their race;
Apollo hunted Daphne so
Only that she might laurel grow;
And Pan did after Syrinx speed
Not as a nymph, but for a reed.

What wondrous life in this I lead!
Ripe apples drop about my head;
The luscious clusters of the vine
Upon my mouth do crush their wine;
The nectarine and curious peach
Into my hands themselves do reach;
Stumbling on melons, as I pass,
Ensnared with flowers, I fall on grass.

Meanwhile the mind from pleasure less
Withdraws into its happiness;
The mind, that ocean where each kind
Does straight its own resemblance find;
Yet it creates, transcending these,
Far other worlds, and other seas;
Annihilating all that's made
To a green thought in a green shade.

Here at the fountain's sliding foot,
Or at some fruit-tree's mossy root,
Casting the body's vest aside,
My soul into the boughs does glide;
There, like a bird, it sits and sings,
Then whets and combs its silver wings,
And, till prepared for longer flight,
Waves in its plumes the various light.

Such was that happy Garden-state
While man there walk'd without a mate:
After a place so pure and sweet,
What other help could yet be meet!
But 'twas beyond a mortal's share
To wander solitary there:
Two paradises 'twere in one,
To live in Paradise alone.

How well the skilful gard'ner drew
Of flowers and herbs this dial new!
Where, from above, the milder sun
Does through a fragrant zodiac run:
And, as it works, th' industrious bee
Computes its time as well as we.
How could such sweet and wholesome hours
Be reckon'd, but with herbs and flowers!

360.   *Bermudas*

WHERE the remote Bermudas ride
    In the ocean's bosom unespied,
From a small boat that row'd along
The listening woods received this song:

    'What should we do but sing His praise
That led us through the watery maze
Unto an isle so long unknown,
And yet far kinder than our own?
Where He the huge sea-monsters wracks,
That lift the deep upon their backs,
He lands us on a grassy stage,
Safe from the storms' and prelates' rage:
He gave us this eternal Spring
Which here enamels everything,
And sends the fowls to us in care
On daily visits through the air:
He hangs in shades the orange bright
Like golden lamps in a green night,
And does in the pomegranates close
Jewels more rich than Ormus shows:
He makes the figs our mouths to meet
And throws the melons at our feet;
But apples plants of such a price,
No tree could ever bear them twice.
With cedars chosen by His hand
From Lebanon He stores the land;
And makes the hollow seas that roar
Proclaim the ambergris on shore.
He cast (of which we rather boast)
The Gospel's pearl upon our coast;
And in these rocks for us did frame
A temple where to sound His name.

O, let our voice His praise exalt
Till it arrive at Heaven's vault,
Which thence (perhaps) rebounding may
Echo beyond the Mexique bay!'

Thus sung they in the English boat
A holy and a cheerful note:
And all the way, to guide their chime,
With falling oars they kept the time.

361.   *An Epitaph*

ENOUGH; and leave the rest to Fame!
'Tis to commend her, but to name.
Courtship which, living, she declined,
When dead, to offer were unkind:
Nor can the truest wit, or friend,
Without detracting, her commend.

To say—she lived a virgin chaste
In this age loose and all unlaced;
Nor was, when vice is so allowed,
Of virtue or ashamed or proud;
That her soul was on Heaven so bent,
No minute but it came and went;
That, ready her last debt to pay,
She summ'd her life up every day;
Modest as morn, as mid-day bright,
Gentle as evening, cool as night:
—'Tis true; but all too weakly said.
'Twas more significant, she 's dead.

HENRY VAUGHAN

1621–1695

362.   ***The Retreat***

H APPY those early days, when I
   Shin'd in my Angel-infancy!
Before I understood this place
Appointed for my second race,
Or taught my soul to fancy aught
But a white celestial thought:
When yet I had not walk'd above
A mile or two from my first Love,
And looking back—at that short space—
Could see a glimpse of His bright face:
When on some gilded cloud, or flow'r,
My gazing soul would dwell an hour,
And in those weaker glories spy
Some shadows of eternity:
Before I taught my tongue to wound
My Conscience with a sinful sound,
Or had the black art to dispense
A several sin to ev'ry sense,
But felt through all this fleshly dress
Bright shoots of everlastingness.

O how I long to travel back,
And tread again that ancient track!
That I might once more reach that plain
Where first I left my glorious train;
From whence th' enlighten'd spirit sees
That shady City of Palm-trees.
But ah! my soul with too much stay
Is drunk, and staggers in the way!
Some men a forward motion love,
But I by backward steps would move;
And when this dust falls to the urn,
In that state I came, return.

363.   *Peace*

MY soul, there is a country
    Far beyond the stars,
Where stands a wingéd sentry
    All skilful in the wars:
There, above noise and danger,
    Sweet Peace sits crown'd with smiles,
And One born in a manger
    Commands the beauteous files.
He is thy gracious Friend,
    And—O my soul, awake!—
Did in pure love descend
    To die here for thy sake.
If thou canst get but thither,
    There grows the flower of Peace,
The Rose that cannot wither,
    Thy fortress, and thy ease.
Leave then thy foolish ranges;
    For none can thee secure
But One who never changes—
    Thy God, thy life, thy cure.

364.   *The Timber*

SURE thou didst flourish once! and many springs,
    Many bright mornings, much dew, many showers,
Pass'd o'er thy head; many light hearts and wings,
    Which now are dead, lodg'd in thy living bowers.

And still a new succession sings and flies;
    Fresh groves grow up, and their green branches shoot
Towards the old and still enduring skies,
    While the low violet thrives at their root.

But thou beneath the sad and heavy line
    Of death, doth waste all senseless, cold, and dark;

Where not so much as dreams of light may shine,
　　Nor any thought of greenness, leaf, or bark.

And yet—as if some deep hate and dissent,
　　Bred in thy growth betwixt high winds and thee,
Were still alive—thou dost great storms resent
　　Before they come, and know'st how near they be.

Else all at rest thou liest, and the fierce breath
　　Of tempests can no more disturb thy ease;
But this thy strange resentment after death
　　Means only those who broke—in life—thy peace.

365.　　　*Friends Departed*

THEY are all gone into the world of light!
　　And I alone sit ling'ring here;
Their very memory is fair and bright,
　　And my sad thoughts doth clear.

It glows and glitters in my cloudy breast,
　　Like stars upon some gloomy grove,
Or those faint beams in which this hill is drest
　　After the sun's remove.

I see them walking in an air of glory,
　　Whose light doth trample on my days:
My days, which are at best but dull and hoary,
　　Mere glimmering and decays.

O holy Hope! and high Humility,
　　High as the heavens above!
These are your walks, and you have show'd them me,
　　To kindle my cold love.

Dear, beauteous Death! the jewel of the Just,
　　Shining nowhere, but in the dark;
What mysteries do lie beyond thy dust,
　　Could man outlook that mark!

He that hath found some fledg'd bird's nest may know,
    At first sight, if the bird be flown;
But what fair well or grove he sings in now,
    That is to him unknown.

And yet as Angels in some brighter dreams
    Call to the soul, when man doth sleep:
So some strange thoughts transcend our wonted themes,
    And into glory peep.

If a star were confined into a tomb,
    Her captive flames must needs burn there;
But when the hand that lock'd her up gives room,
    She'll shine through all the sphere.

O Father of eternal life, and all
    Created glories under Thee!
Resume Thy spirit from this world of thrall
    Into true liberty.

Either disperse these mists, which blot and fill
    My perspective still as they pass:
Or else remove me hence unto that hill,
    Where I shall need no glass.

JOHN BUNYAN

1628–1688

366.   *The Shepherd Boy Sings*
in the Valley of Humiliation

HE that is down needs fear no fall,
    He that is low, no pride;
He that is humble ever shall
    Have God to be his guide.

I am content with what I have,
    Little be it or much:

And, Lord, contentment still I crave,
    Because Thou savest such.

Fullness to such a burden is
    That go on pilgrimage:
Here little, and hereafter bliss,
    Is best from age to age.

BALLADS AND SONGS BY UNKNOWN AUTHORS

367.   *Thomas the Rhymer*

TRUE Thomas lay on Huntlie bank;
    A ferlie he spied wi' his e'e;
And there he saw a ladye bright
    Come riding down by the Eildon Tree.

Her skirt was o' the grass-green silk,
    Her mantle o' the velvet fyne;
At ilka tett o' her horse's mane,
    Hung fifty siller bells and nine.

True Thomas he pu'd aff his cap,
    And louted low down on his knee
'Hail to thee Mary, Queen of Heaven!
    For thy peer on earth could never be.'

'O no, O no, Thomas,' she said,
    'That name does not belang to me;
I'm but the Queen o' fair Elfland,
    That am hither come to visit thee.

'Harp and carp, Thomas,' she said;
    'Harp and carp along wi' me;

367. ferlie] marvel.   tett] tuft, lock. harp and carp] play and recite (as a minstrel).

And if ye dare to kiss my lips,
    Sure of your bodie I will be.'

'Betide me weal; betide me woe,
    That weird shall never daunten me.'
Syne he has kiss'd her rosy lips,
    All underneath the Eildon Tree.

'Now ye maun go wi' me,' she said,
    'True Thomas, ye maun go wi' me;
And ye maun serve me seven years,
    Thro' weal or woe as may chance to be.'

She 's mounted on her milk-white steed,
    She 's ta'en true Thomas up behind;
And aye, whene'er her bridle rang,
    The steed gaed swifter than the wind.

O they rade on, and farther on,
    The steed gaed swifter than the wind;
Until they reach'd a desert wide,
    And living land was left behind.

'Light down, light down now, true Thomas,
    And lean your head upon my knee;
Abide ye there a little space,
    And I will show you ferlies three.

'O see ye not yon narrow road,
    So thick beset wi' thorns and briers?
That is the Path of Righteousness,
    Though after it but few inquires.

'And see ye not yon braid, braid road,
    That lies across the lily leven?
That is the Path of Wickedness,
    Though some call it the Road to Heaven.

leven] ? lawn.

'And see ye not yon bonny road
        That winds about the fernie brae?
That is the Road to fair Elfland,
        Where thou and I this night maun gae.

'But, Thomas, ye sall haud your tongue,
        Whatever ye may hear or see;
For speak ye word in Elfyn-land,
        Ye'll ne'er win back to your ain countrie.'

O they rade on, and farther on,
        And they waded rivers abune the knee;
And they saw neither sun nor moon,
        But they heard the roaring of the sea.

It was mirk, mirk night, there was nae starlight,
        They waded thro' red blude to the knee;
For a' the blude that 's shed on the earth
        Rins through the springs o' that countrie.

Syne they came to a garden green,
        And she pu'd an apple frae a tree:
'Take this for thy wages, true Thomas;
        It will give thee the tongue that can never lee.'

'My tongue is my ain,' true Thomas he said;
        'A gudely gift ye wad gie to me!
I neither dought to buy or sell
        At fair or tryst where I might be.

'I dought neither speak to prince or peer,
        Nor ask of grace from fair ladye!'—
'Now haud thy peace, Thomas,' she said,
        'For as I say, so must it be.'

He has gotten a coat of the even cloth,
        And a pair o' shoon of the velvet green;
And till seven years were gane and past,
        True Thomas on earth was never seen.

dought] could.

368.   ***Sir Patrick Spens***

I. The Sailing

THE king sits in Dunfermline town
    Drinking the blude-red wine;
'O whare will I get a skeely skipper
        To sail this new ship o' mine?'

O up and spak an eldern knight,
        Sat at the king's right knee;
'Sir Patrick Spens is the best sailor
        That ever sail'd the sea.'

Our king has written a braid letter,
        And seal'd it with his hand,
And sent it to Sir Patrick Spens,
        Was walking on the strand.

'To Noroway, to Noroway,
        To Noroway o'er the faem;
The king's daughter o' Noroway,
        'Tis thou must bring her hame.'

The first word that Sir Patrick read
        So loud, loud laugh'd he;
The neist word that Sir Patrick read
        The tear blinded his e'e.

'O wha is this has done this deed
        And tauld the king o' me,
To send us out, at this time o' year,
        To sail upon the sea?

skeely] skilful.

'Be it wind, be it weet, be it hail, be it sleet,
    Our ship must sail the faem;
The king's daughter o' Noroway,
    'Tis we must fetch her hame.'

They hoysed their sails on Monenday morn
    Wi' a' the speed they may;
They hae landed in Noroway
    Upon a Wodensday.

II. The Return

'Mak ready, mak ready, my merry men a':
    Our gude ship sails the morn.'
'Now ever alack, my master dear,
    I fear a deadly storm.

'I saw the new moon late yestreen
    Wi' the auld moon in her arm;
And if we gang to sea, master,
    I fear we'll come to harm.'

They hadna sail'd a league, a league,
    A league but barely three,
When the lift grew dark, and the wind blew loud,
    And gurly grew the sea.

The ankers brak, and the topmast lap,
    It was sic a deadly storm:
And the waves cam owre the broken ship
    Till a' her sides were torn.

'Go fetch a web o' the silken claith,
    Another o' the twine,
And wap them into our ship's side,
    And let nae the sea come in.'

lift] sky.   lap] sprang.

They fetch'd a web o' the silken claith,
    Another o' the twine,
And they wapp'd them round that gude ship's side,
    But still the sea came in.

O laith, laith were our gude Scots lords
    To wet their cork-heel'd shoon;
But lang or a' the play was play'd
    They wat their hats aboon.

And mony was the feather bed
    That flatter'd on the faem;
And mony was the gude lord's son
    That never mair cam hame.

O lang, lang may the ladies sit,
    Wi' their fans into their hand,
Before they see Sir Patrick Spens
    Come sailing to the strand!

And lang, lang may the maidens sit
    Wi' their gowd kames in their hair,
A-waiting for their ain dear loves!
    For them they'll see nae mair.

Half-owre, half-owre to Aberdour,
    'Tis fifty fathoms deep;
And there lies gude Sir Patrick Spens,
    Wi' the Scots lords at his feet!

369. *The Lass of Lochroyan*

'O WHA will shoe my bonny foot?
    And wha will glove my hand?
And wha will bind my middle jimp
    Wi' a lang, lang linen band?

368. flatter'd] tossed afloat. kames] combs. *369.* jimp] trim.

'O wha will kame my yellow hair,
    With a haw bayberry kame?
And wha will be my babe's father
    Till Gregory come hame?'

'They father, he will shoe thy foot,
    Thy brother will glove thy hand,
Thy mither will bind thy middle jimp
    Wi' a lang, lang linen band.

'Thy sister will kame thy yellow hair,
    Wi' a haw bayberry kame;
The Almighty will be thy babe's father
    Till Gregory come hame.'

'And wha will build a bonny ship,
    And set it on the sea?
For I will go to seek my love,
    My ain love Gregory.'

Up then spak her father dear,
    A wafu' man was he;
'And I will build a bonny ship,
    And set her on the sea.

'And I will build a bonny ship,
    And set her on the sea,
And ye sal gae and seek your love,
    Your ain love Gregory.'

Then he's gart build a bonny ship,
    And set it on the sea,
Wi' four-and-twenty mariners,
    To bear her company.

kame] comb.   haw bayberry] ? a corruption for 'braw
ivory' : or bayberry may = laurel-wood.

ANONYMOUS

O he's gart build a bonny ship,
    To sail on the salt sea;
The mast was o' the beaten gold,
    The sails o' cramoisie.

The sides were o' the gude stout aik,
    The deck o' mountain pine,
The anchor o' the silver shene,
    The ropes o' silken twine.

She hadna sail'd but twenty leagues,
    But twenty leagues and three,
When she met wi' a rank reiver,
    And a' his companie.

'Now are ye Queen of Heaven hie,
    Come to pardon a' our sin?
Or are ye Mary Magdalane,
    Was born at Bethlam?'

'I'm no the Queen of Heaven hie,
    Come to pardon ye your sin,
Nor am I Mary Magdalane,
    Was born in Bethlam.

'But I'm the lass of Lochroyan,
    That's sailing on the sea
To see if I can find my love,
    My ain love Gregory.'

'O see na ye yon bonny bower?
    It 's a' covered owre wi' tin;
When thou hast sail'd it round about,
    Lord Gregory is within.'

cramoisie] crimson.   reiver] robber.

And when she saw the stately tower,
    Shining both clear and bright,
Whilk stood aboon the jawing wave,
    Built on a rock of height,

Says, 'Row the boat, my mariners,
    And bring me to the land,
For yonder I see my love's castle,
    Close by the salt sea strand.'

She sail'd it round, and sail'd it round,
    And loud and loud cried she,
'Now break, now break your fairy charms,
    And set my true-love free.'

She 's ta'en her young son in her arms,
    And to the door she's gane,
And long she knock'd, and sair she ca'd.
    But answer got she nane.

'O open, open, Gregory!
    O open! if ye be within;
For here's the lass of Lochroyan,
    Come far fra kith and kin.

'O open the door, Lord Gregory!
    O open and let me in!
The wind blows loud and cauld, Gregory,
    The rain drops fra my chin.

'The shoe is frozen to my foot,
    The glove unto my hand,
The wet drops fra my yellow hair,
    Na langer dow I stand.'

dow] can.

O up then spak his ill mither,
  —An ill death may she die!
'Ye're no the lass of Lochroyan,
  She 's far out-owre the sea.

'Awa', awa', ye ill woman,
  Ye're no come here for gude;
Ye're but some witch or wil' warlock,
  Or mermaid o' the flood.'

'I am neither witch nor wil' warlock,
  Nor mermaid o' the sea,
But I am Annie of Lochroyan,
  O open the door to me!'

'Gin ye be Annie of Lochroyan,
  As I trow thou binna she,
Now tell me of some love-tokens
  That pass'd 'tween thee and me.'

'O dinna ye mind, love Gregory,
  As we sat at the wine,
We changed the rings frae our fingers?
  And I can shew thee thine.

'O yours was gude, and gude enough,
  But ay the best was mine,
For yours was o' the gude red gowd,
  But mine o' the diamond fine.

'Yours was o' the gude red gowd,
  Mine o' the diamond fine;
Mine was o' the purest troth,
  But thine was false within.'

'If ye be the lass of Lochroyan,
  As I kenna thou be,
Tell me some mair o' the love-tokens
  Pass'd between thee and me.'

ANONYMOUS

'And dinna ye mind, love Gregory!
   As we sat on the hill,
Thou twin'd me o' my maidenheid,
   Right sair against my will?

'Now open the door, love Gregory!
   Open the door! I pray;
For thy young son is in my arms,
   And will be dead ere day.'

'Ye lie, ye lie, ye ill woman,
   So loud I hear ye lie;
For Annie of the Lochroyan
   Is far out-owre the sea.'

Fair Annie turn'd her round about:
   'Weel, sine that it be sae,
May ne'er woman that has borne a son
   Hae a heart sae fu' o' wae!

'Tak down, tak down that mast o' gowd,
   Set up a mast of tree;
It disna become a forsaken lady
   To sail sae royallie.'

When the cock had crawn, and the day did dawn,
   And the sun began to peep,
Up than raise Lord Gregory,
   And sair, sair did he weep.

'O I hae dream'd a dream, mither,
   I wish it may bring good!
That the bonny lass of Lochroyan
   At my bower window stood.

'O I hae dream'd a dream, mither,
   The thought o't gars me greet!
That fair Annie of Lochroyan
   Lay dead at my bed-feet.'

93

'Gin it be for Annie of Lochroyan
    That ye mak a' this mane,
She stood last night at your bower-door,
    But I hae sent her hame.'

'O wae betide ye, ill woman,
    An ill death may ye die!
That wadna open the door yoursell
    Nor yet wad waken me.'

O he 's gane down to yon shore-side,
    As fast as he could dree,
And there he saw fair Annie's bark
    A rowing owre the sea.

'O Annie, Annie,' loud he cried,
    'O Annie, O Annie, bide!'
But ay the mair he cried 'Annie,'
    The braider grew the tide.

'O Annie, Annie, dear Annie,
    Dear Annie, speak to me!'
But ay the louder he gan call,
    The louder roar'd the sea.

The wind blew loud, the waves rose hie
    And dash'd the boat on shore;
Fair Annie's corpse was in the faem,
    The babe rose never more.

Lord Gregory tore his gowden locks
    And made a wafu' moan;
Fair Annie's corpse lay at his feet,
    His bonny son was gone.

'O cherry, cherry was her cheek,
    And gowden was her hair,
And coral, coral was her lips,
    Nane might with her compare.'

Then first he kiss'd her pale, pale cheek,
    And syne he kiss'd her chin,
And syne he kiss'd her wane, wane lips,
    There was na breath within.

'O wae betide my ill mither,
    An ill death may she die!
She turn'd my true-love frae my door,
    Who cam so far to me.

'O wae betide my ill mither,
    An ill death may she die!
She has no been the deid o' ane,
    But she's been the deid of three.'

Then he 's ta'en out a little dart,
    Hung low down by his gore,
He thrust it through and through his heart,
    And words spak never more.

370.   *The Dowie Houms of Yarrow*

LATE at een, drinkin' the wine,
    And ere they paid the lawin',
They set a combat them between,
    To fight it in the dawin'.

'O stay at hame, my noble lord!
    O stay at hame, my marrow!
My cruel brother will you betray,
    On the dowie houms o' Yarrow.'

'O fare ye weel, my lady gay!
    O fare ye weel, my Sarah!
For I maun gae, tho' I ne'er return
    Frae the dowie banks o' Yarrow.'

369. gore] skirt, waist.   *370.* lawin'] reckoning.
marrow] mate, husband or wife.   dowie] doleful
houms] water-meads.

She kiss'd his cheek, she kamed his hair,
    As she had done before, O;
She belted on his noble brand,
    An' he 's awa to Yarrow.

O he 's gane up yon high, high hill—
    I wat he gaed wi' sorrow—
An' in a den spied nine arm'd men,
    I' the dowie houms o' Yarrow.

'O are ye come to drink the wine,
    As ye hae doon before, O?
Or are ye come to wield the brand,
    On the dowie banks o' Yarrow?'

'I am no come to drink the wine,
    As I hae don before, O,
But I am come to wield the brand,
    On the dowie houms o' Yarrow.'

Four he hurt, an' five he slew,
    On the dowie houms o' Yarrow,
Till that stubborn knight came him behind,
    An' ran his body thorrow.

'Gae hame, gae hame, good brother John,
    An' tell your sister Sarah
To come an' lift her noble lord,
    Who's sleepin' sound on Yarrow.'

'Yestreen I dream'd a dolefu' dream;
    I ken'd there wad be sorrow;
I dream'd I pu'd the heather green,
    On the dowie banks o' Yarrow.'

She gaed up yon high, high hill—
    I wat she gaed wi' sorrow—
An' in a den spied nine dead men,
    On the dowie houms o' Yarrow.

She kiss'd his cheek, she kamed his hair,
 As oft she did before, O;
She drank the red blood frae him ran,
 On the dowie houms o' Yarrow.

'O haud your tongue, my douchter dear,
 For what needs a' this sorrow?
I'll wed you on a better lord
 Than him you lost on Yarrow.'

'O haud your tongue, my father dear,
 An' dinna grieve your Sarah;
A better lord was never born
 Than him I lost on Yarrow.'

'Tak hame your ousen, tak hame your kye,
 For they hae bred our sorrow;
I wiss that they had a' gane mad
 When they cam first to Yarrow.'

371.   *Clerk Saunders*

CLERK SAUNDERS and may Margaret
 Walk'd owre yon garden green;
And deep and heavy was the love
 That fell thir twa between.

'A bed, a bed,' Clerk Saunders said,
 'A bed for you and me!'
'Fye na, fye na,' said may Margaret,
 'Till anes we married be!'

'Then I'll take the sword frae my scabbard
 And slowly lift the pin;
And you may swear, and save your aith,
 Ye ne'er let Clerk Saunders in.

'Take you a napkin in your hand,
    And tie up baith your bonnie e'en,
And you may swear, and save your aith,
    Ye saw me na since late yestreen.'

It was about the midnight hour,
    When they asleep were laid,
When in and came her seven brothers,
    Wi' torches burning red:

When in and came her seven brothers,
    Wi' torches burning bright:
They said, 'We hae but one sister,
    And behold her lying with a knight!'

Then out and spake the first o' them,
    'I bear the sword shall gar him die.'
And out and spake the second o' them,
    'His father has nae mair but he.'

And out and spake the third o' them,
    'I wot that they are lovers dear.'
And out and spake the fourth o' them,
    'They hae been in love this mony a year.'

Then out and spake the fifth o' them,
    'It were great sin true love to twain.'
And out and spake the sixth o' them,
    'It were shame to slay a sleeping man.'

Then up and gat the seventh o' them,
    And never a word spake he;
But he has striped his bright brown brand
    Out through Clerk Saunders' fair bodye.

Clerk Saunders he started, and Margaret she turn'd
    Into his arms as asleep she lay;

striped] thrust.

And sad and silent was the night
 That was atween thir twae.

And they lay still and sleepit sound
 Until the day began to daw';
And kindly she to him did say,
 'It is time, true love, you were awa'.'

But he lay still, and sleepit sound,
 Albeit the sun began to sheen;
She look'd atween her and the wa',
 And dull and drowsie were his e'en.

Then in and came her father dear;
 Said, 'Let a' your mourning be;
I'll carry the dead corse to the clay,
 And I'll come back and comfort thee.'

'Comfort weel your seven sons,
 For comforted I will never be:
I ween 'twas neither knave nor loon
 Was in the bower last night wi' me.'

The clinking bell gaed through the town,
 To carry the dead corse to the clay;
And Clerk Saunders stood at may Margaret's window,
 I wot, an hour before the day.

'Are ye sleeping, Marg'ret?' he says,
 'Or are ye waking presentlie?
Give me my faith and troth again,
 I wot, true love, I gied to thee.'

'Your faith and troth ye sall never get,
 Nor our true love sall never twin,
Until ye come within my bower,
 And kiss me cheik and chin.'

twin] part in two.

'My mouth it is full cold, Marg'ret;
       It has the smell, now, of the ground;
And if I kiss thy comely mouth,
       Thy days of life will not be lang.

'O cocks are crowing a merry midnight;
       I wot the wild fowls are boding day;
Give me my faith and troth again,
       And let me fare me on my way.'

'Thy faith and troth thou sallna get,
       And our true love sall never twin,
Until ye tell what comes o' women,
       I wot, who die in strong traivelling?'

'Their beds are made in the heavens high,
       Down at the foot of our good Lord's knee,
Weel set about wi' gillyflowers;
       I wot, sweet company for to see.

'O cocks are crowing a merry midnight;
       I wot the wild fowls are boding day;
The psalms of heaven will soon be sung,
       And I, ere now, will be miss'd away.'

Then she has taken a crystal wand,
       And she has stroken her troth thereon;
She has given it him out at the shot-window,
       Wi' mony a sad sigh and heavy groan.

'I thank ye, Marg'ret; I thank ye, Marg'ret;
       And ay I thank ye heartilie;
Gin ever the dead come for the quick,
       Be sure, Marg'ret, I'll come for thee.'

It 's hosen and shoon, and gown alone,
       She climb'd the wall, and follow'd him,
Until she came to the green forest,
       And there she lost the sight o' him.

'Is there ony room at your head, Saunders?
　　Is there ony room at your feet?
Or ony room at your side, Saunders,
　　Where fain, fain, I wad sleep?'

'There 's nae room at my head, Marg'ret,
　　There 's nae room at my feet;
My bed it is fu' lowly now,
　　Amang the hungry worms I sleep.

'Cauld mould is my covering now,
　　But and my winding-sheet;
The dew it falls nae sooner down
　　Than my resting-place is weet.

'But plait a wand o' bonny birk,
　　And lay it on my breast;
And shed a tear upon my grave,
　　And wish my saul gude rest.'

Then up and crew the red, red cock,
　　And up and crew the gray:
''Tis time, 'tis time, my dear Marg'ret,
　　That you were going away.

'And fair Marg'ret, and rare Marg'ret,
　　And Marg'ret o' veritie,
Gin e'er ye love another man,
　　Ne'er love him as ye did me.'

372. *Fair Annie*

THE reivers they stole Fair Annie,
　　As she walk'd by the sea;
But a noble knight was her ransom soon,
　　Wi' gowd and white monie.

She bided in strangers' land wi' him,
　　And none knew whence she cam;

She lived in the castle wi' her love,
　　But never told her name.

'It 's narrow, narrow, mak your bed,
　　And learn to lie your lane;
For I'm gaun owre the sea, Fair Annie,
　　A braw Bride to bring hame.
Wi' her I will get gowd and gear,
　　Wi' you I ne'er gat nane.'

'But wha will bake my bridal bread,
　　Or brew my bridal ale?
And wha will welcome my bright Bride,
　　That I bring owre the dale?'

'It 's I will bake your bridal bread,
　　And brew your bridal ale;
And I will welcome your bright Bride,
　　That you bring owre the dale.'

'But she that welcomes my bright Bride
　　Maun gang like maiden fair;
She maun lace on her robe sae jimp,
　　And comely braid her hair.

'Bind up, bind up your yellow hair,
　　And tie it on your neck;
And see you look as maiden-like
　　As the day that first we met.'

'O how can I gang maiden-like,
　　When maiden I am nane?
Have I not borne six sons to thee,
　　And am wi' child again?'

'I'll put cooks into my kitchen,
　　And stewards in my hall,

jimp] trim.

ANONYMOUS

And I'll have bakers for my bread,
    And brewers for my ale;
But you're to welcome my bright Bride,
    That I bring owre the dale.'

Three months and a day were gane and past,
    Fair Annie she gat word
That her love's ship was come at last,
    Wi' his bright young Bride aboard.

She's ta'en her young son in her arms,
    Anither in her hand;
And she's gane up to the highest tower,
    Looks over sea and land.

'Come doun, come doun, my mother dear,
    Come aff the castle wa'!
I fear if langer ye stand there,
    Ye 'll let yoursell doun fa.'

She's ta'en a cake o' the best bread,
    A stoup o' the best wine,
And a' the keys upon her arm,
    And to the yett is gane.

'O ye're welcome hame, my ain gude lord,
    To your castles and your towers;
Ye're welcome hame, my ain gude lord,
    To your ha's, but and your bowers.
And welcome to your hame, fair lady!
    For a' that 's here is yours.'

'O whatna lady 's that, my lord,
    That welcomes you and me?
Gin I be lang about this place,
    Her friend I mean to be.'

yett] gate.

Fair Annie served the lang tables
  Wi' the white bread and the wine;
But ay she drank the wan water
  To keep her colour fine.

And she gaed by the first table,
  And smiled upon them a';
But ere she reach'd the second table,
  The tears began to fa'.

She took a napkin lang and white,
  And hung it on a pin;
It was to wipe away the tears,
  As she gaed out and in.

When bells were rung and mass was sung,
  And a' men bound for bed,
The bridegroom and the bonny Bride
  In ae chamber were laid.

Fair Annie 's ta'en a harp in her hand,
  To harp thir twa asleep;
But ay, as she harpit and she sang,
  Fu' sairly did she weep.

'O gin my sons were seven rats,
  Rinnin' on the castle wa',
And I mysell a great grey cat,
  I soon wad worry them a'!

'O gin my sons were seven hares,
  Rinnin' owre yon lily lea,
And I mysell a good greyhound,
  Soon worried they a' should be!'

Then out and spak the bonny young Bride,
  In bride-bed where she lay:

'That 's like my sister Annie,' she says;
 'Wha is it doth sing and play?
'I'll put on my gown,' said the new-come Bride,
 'And my shoes upon my feet;
I will see wha doth sae sadly sing,
 And what is it gars her greet.

'What ails you, what ails you, my housekeeper,
 That ye mak sic a mane?
Has ony wine-barrel cast its girds,
 Or is a' your white bread gane?'

'It isna because my wine is spilt,
 Or that my white bread 's gane;
But because I've lost my true love's love,
 And he 's wed to anither ane.'

'Noo tell me wha was your father?' she says,
 'Noo tell me wha was your mother?
And had ye ony sister?' she says,
 'And had ye ever a brother?'

'The Earl of Wemyss was my father,
 The Countess of Wemyss my mother,
Young Elinor she was my sister dear,
 And Lord John he was my brother.'

'If the Earl of Wemyss was your father,
 I wot sae was he mine;
And it 's O my sister Annie!
 Your love ye sallna tyne.

'Tak your husband, my sister dear;
 You ne'er were wrang'd for me,
Beyond a kiss o' his merry mouth
 As we cam owre the sea.

tyne] lose.

'Seven ships, loaded weel,
    Cam owre the sea wi' me;
Ane o' them will tak me hame,
    And six I'll gie to thee.'

373.   *Edward, Edward*

'WHY does your brand sae drop wi' blude,
    Edward, Edward?
Why does your brand sae drop wi' blude,
    And why sae sad gang ye, O?'
'O I hae kill'd my hawk sae gude,
    Mither, mither;
O I hae kill'd my hawk sae gude,
    And I had nae mair but he, O.'

'Your hawk's blude was never sae red,
    Edward, Edward;
Your hawk's blude was never sae red,
    My dear son, I tell thee, O.'
'O I hae kill'd my red-roan steed,
    Mither, mither;
O I hae kill'd my red-roan steed,
    That erst was sae fair and free, O.'

'Your steed was auld, and ye hae got mair,
    Edward, Edward;
Your steed was auld, and ye hae got mair;
    Some other dule ye dree, O.'
'O I hae kill'd my father dear,
    Mither, mither;
O I hae kill'd my father dear,
    Alas, and wae is me, O!'

373. dule ye dree] grief you suffer.

'And whatten penance will ye dree for that,
    Edward, Edward?
Whatten penance will ye dree for that?
    My dear son, now tell me, O.'
'I'll set my feet in yonder boat,
    Mither, mither;
I'll set my feet in yonder boat,
    And I'll fare over the sea, O.'

'And what will ye do wi' your tow'rs and your ha',
    Edward, Edward?
And what will ye do wi' your tow'rs and your ha',
    That were sae fair to see, O?'
'I'll let them stand till they doun fa',
    Mither, mither;
I'll let them stand till they doun fa',
    For here never mair maun I be, O.'

'And what will ye leave to your bairns and your wife,
    Edward, Edward?
And what will ye leave to your bairns and your wife,
    When ye gang owre the sea, O?'
'The warld's room: let them beg through life,
    Mither, mither;
The warld's room: let them beg through life;
    For them never mair will I see, O.'

'And what will ye leave to your ain mither dear,
    Edward, Edward?
And what will ye leave to your ain mither dear,
    My dear son, now tell me, O?'
'The curse of hell frae me sall ye bear,
    Mither, mither;
The curse of hell frae me sall ye bear:
    Sic counsels ye gave to me, O!'

374. *Edom o' Gordon*

IT fell about the Martinmas,
 When the wind blew shrill and cauld,
Said Edom o' Gordon to his men,
 'We maun draw to a hauld.

'And what a hauld sall we draw to,
 My merry men and me?
We will gae to the house o' the Rodes,
 To see that fair ladye.'

The lady stood on her castle wa',
 Beheld baith dale and down;
There she was ware of a host of men
 Cam riding towards the town.

'O see ye not, my merry men a',
 O see ye not what I see?
Methinks I see a host of men;
 I marvel wha they be.'

She ween'd it had been her lovely lord,
 As he cam riding hame;
It was the traitor, Edom o' Gordon,
 Wha reck'd nae sin nor shame.

She had nae sooner buskit hersell,
 And putten on her gown,
But Edom o' Gordon an' his men
 Were round about the town.

They had nae sooner supper set,
 Nae sooner said the grace,
But Edom o' Gordon an' his men
 Were lighted about the place.

town] stead. buskit] attired.

The lady ran up to her tower-head,
    Sae fast as she could hie,
To see if by her fair speeches
    She could wi' him agree.

'Come doun to me, ye lady gay,
    Come doun, come doun to me;
This night sall ye lig within mine arms,
    To-morrow my bride sall be.'

'I winna come down, ye fals Gordon,
    I winna come down to thee;
I winna forsake my ain dear lord,
    That is sae far frae me.'

'Gie owre your house, ye lady fair,
    Gie owre your house to me;
Or I sall brenn yoursel therein,
    But and your babies three.'

'I winna gie owre, ye fals Gordon,
    To nae sic traitor as yee;
And if ye brenn my ain dear babes,
    My lord sall mak ye dree.

'Now reach my pistol, Glaud, my man,
    And charge ye weel my gun;
For, but an I pierce that bluidy butcher,
    My babes, we been undone!'

She stood upon her castle wa',
    And let twa bullets flee:
She miss'd that bluidy butcher's heart,
    And only razed his knee.

'Set fire to the house!' quo' fals Gordon,
    All wud wi' dule and ire:

wud] mad.

'Fals lady, ye sall rue this deid
　　As ye brenn in the fire!'

'Wae worth, wae worth ye, Jock, my man!
　　I paid ye weel your fee;
Why pu' ye out the grund-wa' stane,
　　Lets in the reek to me?

'And e'en wae worth ye, Jock, my man!
　　I paid ye weel your hire;
Why pu' ye out the grund-wa' stane,
　　To me lets in the fire?'

'Ye paid me weel my hire, ladye,
　　Ye paid me weel my fee:
But now I'm Edom o' Gordon's man—
　　Maun either do or die.'

O then bespake her little son,
　　Sat on the nurse's knee:
Says, 'Mither dear, gie owre this house,
　　For the reek it smithers me.'

'I wad gie a' my gowd, my bairn,
　　Sae wad I a' my fee,
For ae blast o' the western wind,
　　To blaw the reek frae thee.'

O then bespake her dochter dear—
　　She was baith jimp and sma':
'O row me in a pair o' sheets,
　　And tow me owre the wa'!'

They row'd her in a pair o' sheets,
　　And tow'd her owre the wa';
But on the point o' Gordon's spear
　　She gat a deadly fa'.

grund-wa] groundwall.　jimp] slender, trim.
row] roll, wrap.

ANONYMOUS

O bonnie, bonnie was her mouth,
    And cherry were her cheiks,
And clear, clear was her yellow hair,
    Whereon the red blood dreips.

Then wi' his spear he turn'd her owre;
    O gin her face was wane!
He said, 'Ye are the first that e'er
    I wish'd alive again.'

He turn'd her owre and owre again;
    O gin her skin was white!
'I might hae spared that bonnie face
    To hae been some man's delight.

'Busk and boun, my merry men a',
    For ill dooms I do guess;
I canna look in that bonnie face
    As it lies on the grass.'

'Wha looks to freits, my master dear,
    It 's freits will follow them;
Let it ne'er be said that Edom o' Gordon
    Was daunted by a dame.'

But when the lady saw the fire
    Come flaming owre her head,
She wept, and kiss'd her children twain,
    Says, 'Bairns, we been but dead.'
The Gordon then his bugle blew,
    And said, 'Awa', awa'!
This house o' the Rodes is a' in a flame;
    I hauld it time to ga'.'

And this way lookit her ain dear lord,
    As he cam owre the lea;

Busk and boun] trim up and prepare to go.
freits] ill omens.

He saw his castle a' in a lowe,
    As far as he could see.

The sair, O sair, his mind misgave,
    And all his heart was wae:
'Put on, put on, my wighty men,
    Sae fast as ye can gae.

'Put on, put on, my wighty men,
    Sae fast as ye can drie!
For he that 's hindmost o' the thrang
    Sall ne'er get good o' me.'

Then some they rade, and some they ran,
    Out-owre the grass and bent;
But ere the foremost could win up,
    Baith lady and babes were brent.

And after the Gordon he is gane,
    Sae fast as he might drie;
And soon i' the Gordon's foul heart's blude
    He 's wroken his dear ladye.

375. *The Queen's Marie*

MARIE HAMILTON 's to the kirk gane,
    Wi' ribbons in her hair;
The King thought mair o' Marie Hamilton
    Than ony that were there.

Marie Hamilton 's to the kirk gane
    Wi' ribbons on her breast;
The King thought mair o' Marie Hamilton
    Than he listen'd to the priest.

Marie Hamilton 's to the kirk gane,
    Wi' gloves upon her hands;

374. lowe] flame. wighty] stout, doughty.
wroken] avenged.

The King thought mair o' Marie Hamilton
    Than the Queen and a' her lands.

She hadna been about the King's court
    A month, but barely one,
Till she was beloved by a' the King's court
    And the King the only man.

She hadna been about the King's court
    A month, but barely three,
Till frae the King's court Marie Hamilton,
    Marie Hamilton durstna be.

The King is to the Abbey gane,
    To pu' the Abbey tree,
To scale the babe frae Marie's heart;
    But the thing it wadna be.

O she has row'd it in her apron,
    And set it on the sea—
'Gae sink ye or swim ye, bonny babe,
    Ye'se get nae mair o' me.'

Word is to the kitchen gane,
    And word is to the ha',
And word is to the noble room
    Amang the ladies a',
That Marie Hamilton 's brought to bed,
    And the bonny babe 's miss'd and awa'.

Scarcely had she lain down again,
    And scarcely fa'en asleep,
When up and started our gude Queen
    Just at her bed-feet;
Saying—'Marie Hamilton, where 's your babe?
    For I am sure I heard it greet.'

row'd] rolled, wrapped.

'O no, O no, my noble Queen!
  Think no sic thing to be;
'Twas but a stitch into my side,
  And sair it troubles me!'

'Get up, get up, Marie Hamilton:
  Get up and follow me;
For I am going to Edinburgh town,
  A rich wedding for to see.'

O slowly, slowly rase she up,
  And slowly put she on;
And slowly rade she out the way
  Wi' mony a weary groan.

The Queen was clad in scarlet,
  Her merry maids all in green;
And every town that they cam to,
  They took Marie for the Queen.

'Ride hooly, hooly, gentlemen,
  Ride hooly now wi' me!
For never, I am sure, a wearier burd
  Rade in your companie.'—

But little wist Marie Hamilton,
  When she rade on the brown,
That she was gaen to Edinburgh town,
  And a' to be put down.

'Why weep ye so, ye burgess wives,
  Why look ye so on me?
O I am going to Edinburgh town,
  A rich wedding to see.'

When she gaed up the tolbooth stairs,
  The corks frae her heels did flee;

greet] cry. hooly] gently.

114

And lang or e'er she cam down again,
    She was condemn'd to die.

When she cam to the Netherbow port,
    She laugh'd loud laughters three;
But when she came to the gallows foot
    The tears blinded her e'e.

'Yestreen the Queen had four Maries,
    The night she'll hae but three;
There was Marie Seaton, and Marie Beaton,
    And Marie Carmichael, and me.

'O often have I dress'd my Queen
    And put gowd upon her hair;
But now I've gotten for my reward
    The gallows to be my share.

'Often have I dress'd my Queen
    And often made her bed;
But now I've gotten for my reward
    The gallows tree to tread.

'I charge ye all, ye mariners,
    When ye sail owre the faem,
Let neither my father nor mother get wit
    But that I'm coming hame.

'I charge ye all, ye mariners,
    That sail upon the sea,
That neither my father nor mother get wit
    The dog's death I'm to die.

'For if my father and mother got wit,
    And my bold brethren three,
O mickle wad be the gude red blude
    This day wad be spilt for me!

'O little did my mother ken,
 The day she cradled me,
The lands I was to travel in
 Or the death I was to die!'

376.   *Binnorie*

THERE were twa sisters sat in a bour;
 Binnorie, O Binnorie!
There cam a knight to be their wooer,
 By the bonnie milldams o' Binnorie.

He courted the eldest with glove and ring,
 Binnorie, O Binnorie!
But he lo'ed the youngest abune a' thing.
 By the bonnie milldams o' Binnorie.

The eldest she was vexéd sair,
 Binnorie, O Binnorie!
And sair envíed her sister fair.
 By the bonnie milldams o' Binnorie.

Upon a morning fair and clear,
 Binnorie, O Binnorie!
She cried upon her sister dear:
 By the bonnie milldams o' Binnorie.

'O sister, sister tak my hand,
 Binnorie, O Binnorie!
And let 's go down to the river-strand.'
 By the bonnie milldams o' Binnorie.

She 's ta'en her by the lily hand,
 Binnorie, O Binnorie!
And led her down to the river-strand.
 By the bonnie milldams o' Binnorie.

The youngest stood upon a stane,
　　Binnorie, O Binnorie!
The eldest cam and push'd her in.
　　By the bonnie milldams o' Binnorie.

'O sister, sister reach your hand!
　　Binnorie, O Binnorie!
And ye sall be heir o' half my land:
　　By the bonnie milldams o' Binnorie.

'O sister, reach me but your glove!
　　Binnorie, O Binnorie!
And sweet William sall be your love.'
　　By the bonnie milldams o' Binnorie.

Sometimes she sank, sometimes she swam,
　　Binnorie, O Binnorie!
Until she cam to the miller's dam.
　　By the bonnie milldams o' Binnorie.

Out then cam the miller's son,
　　Binnorie, O Binnorie!
And saw the fair maid soummin' in.
　　By the bonnie milldams o' Binnorie.

'O father, father draw your dam!
　　Binnorie, O Binnorie!
There's either a mermaid or a milk-white swan.'
　　By the bonnie milldams o' Binnorie.

The miller hasted and drew his dam,
　　Binnorie, O Binnorie!
And there he found a drown'd womán.
　　By the bonnie milldams o' Binnorie.

soummin'] swimming.

You couldna see her middle sma',
  Binnorie, O Binnorie!
Her gowden girdle was sae braw.
  By the bonnie milldams o' Binnorie.

You couldna see her lily feet,
  Binnorie, O Binnorie!
Her gowden fringes were sae deep.
  By the bonnie milldams o' Binnorie.

All amang her yellow hair
  Binnorie, O Binnorie!
A string o' pearls was twisted rare.
  By the bonnie milldams o' Binnorie.

You couldna see her fingers sma',
  Binnorie, O Binnorie!
Wi' diamond rings they were cover'd a'.
  By the bonnie milldams o' Binnorie.

And by there cam a harper fine,
  Binnorie, O Binnorie!
That harpit to the king at dine.
  By the bonnie milldams o' Binnorie.

And when he look'd that lady on,
  Binnorie, O Binnorie!
He sigh'd and made a heavy moan.
  By the bonnie milldams o' Binnorie.

He 's made a harp of her breast-bane,
  Binnorie, O Binnorie!
Whose sound wad melt a heart of stane.
  By the bonnie milldams o' Binnorie.

He 's ta'en three locks o' her yellow hair,
  Binnorie, O Binnorie!

And wi' them strung his harp sae rare.
 By the bonnie milldams o' Binnorie.

He went into her father's hall,
 Binnorie, O Binnorie!
And there was the court assembled all.
 By the bonnie milldams o' Binnorie.

He laid his harp upon a stane,
 Binnorie, O Binnorie!
And straight it began to play by lane.
 By the bonnie milldams o' Binnorie.

'O yonder sits my father, the King,
 Binnorie, O Binnorie!
And yonder sits my mother, the Queen;
 By the bonnie milldams o' Binnorie.

'And yonder stands my brother Hugh,
 Binnorie, O Binnorie!
And by him my William, sweet and true.'
 By the bonnie milldams o' Binnorie.

But the last tune that the harp play'd then—
 Binnorie, O Binnorie!
Was, 'Woe to my sister, false Helén!'
 By the bonnie milldams o' Binnorie.

377. *The Bonnie House o' Airlie*

IT fell on a day, and a bonnie simmer day,
 When green grew aits and barley,
That there fell out a great dispute
 Between Argyll and Airlie.

ANONYMOUS

Argyll has raised an hunder men,
  An hunder harness'd rarely,
And he 's awa' by the back of Dunkell,
  To plunder the castle of Airlie.

Lady Ogilvie looks o'er her bower-window,
  And O but she looks warely!
And there she spied the great Argyll,
  Come to plunder the bonnie house of Airlie.

'Come down, come down, my Lady Ogilvie,
  Come down and kiss me fairly—'
'O I winna kiss the fause Argyll,
  If he shouldna leave a standing stane in Airlie.'

He hath taken her by the left shoulder,
  Says, 'Dame, where lies thy dowry?'
'O it 's east and west yon wan water side,
  And it 's down by the banks of the Airlie.'

They hae sought it up, they hae sought it down,
  They hae sought it maist severely,
Till they fand it in the fair plum-tree
  That shines on the bowling-green of Airlie.

He hath taken her by the middle sae small,
  And O but she grat sairly!
And laid her down by the bonnie burn-side,
  Til they plunder'd the castle of Airlie.

'Gif my gude lord war here this night,
  As he is with King Charlie,
Neither you, nor ony ither Scottish lord,
  Durst avow to the plundering of Airlie.

'Gif my gude lord war now at hame,
  As he is with his king,
There durst nae a Campbell in a' Argyll
  Set fit on Airlie green.

'Ten bonnie sons I have borne unto him,
  The eleventh ne'er saw his daddy;
But though I had an hunder mair,
  I'd gie them a' to King Charlie!'

378. *The Wife of Usher's Well*

THERE lived a wife at Usher's well,
  And a wealthy wife was she;
She had three stout and stalwart sons,
  And sent them o'er the sea.

They hadna been a week from her,
  A week but barely ane,
When word came to the carline wife
  That her three sons were gane.

They hadna been a week from her,
  A week but barely three,
When word came to the carline wife
  That her sons she'd never see.

'I wish the wind may never cease,
  Nor fashes in the flood,
Till my three sons come hame to me,
  In earthly flesh and blood!'

It fell about the Martinmas,
  When nights are lang and mirk,
The carline wife's three sons came hame,
  And their hats were o' the birk.

It neither grew in syke nor ditch,
  Nor yet in ony sheugh;
But at the gates o' Paradise
  That birk grew fair eneugh.

fashes] troubles.   syke] marsh.   sheugh] trench.

'Blow up the fire, my maidens!
　　Bring water from the well!
For a' my house shall feast this night,
　　Since my three sons are well.'

And she has made to them a bed,
　　She's made it large and wide;
And she 's ta'en her mantle her about,
　　Sat down at the bedside.

Up then crew the red, red cock,
　　And up and crew the gray;
The eldest to the youngest said,
　　'''Tis time we were away.'

The cock he hadna craw'd but once,
　　And clapp'd his wings at a',
When the youngest to the eldest said,
　　'Brother, we must awa'.

'The cock doth craw, the day doth daw,
　　The channerin' worm doth chide;
Gin we be miss'd out o' our place,
　　A sair pain we maun bide.'

'Lie still, lie still but a little wee while,
　　Lie still but if we may;
Gin my mother should miss us when she wakes,
　　She'll go mad ere it be day.'

'Fare ye weel, my mother dear!
　　Fareweel to barn and byre!
And fare ye weel, the bonny lass
　　That kindles my mother's fire!'

378. channerin'] fretting.

122

379. *The Three Ravens*

THERE were three ravens sat on a tree,
They were as black as they might be.

The one of them said to his make,
'Where shall we our breakfast take?'

'Down in yonder greené field
There lies a knight slain under his shield;

'His hounds they lie down at his feet,
So well they can their master keep;

'His hawks they flie so eagerly,
There 's no fowl dare come him nigh.'

Down there comes a fallow doe
As great with young as she might goe.

She lift up his bloudy head
And kist his wounds that were so red.

She gat him up upon her back
And carried him to earthen lake.

She buried him before the prime,
She was dead herself ere evensong time.

God send every gentleman
Such hounds, such hawks, and such a leman.

380. *The Twa Corbies*
Scottish Version

AS I was walking all alane
I heard twa corbies making a mane:
The tane unto the tither did say,
'Whar sall we gang and dine the day?'

379. make] mate.   *380.* corbies] ravens.

123

'—In behint yon auld fail dyke
I wot there lies a new-slain knight;
And naebody kens that he lies there
But his hawk, his hound, and his lady fair.
'His hound is to the hunting gane,
His hawk to fetch the wild-fowl hame,
His lady's ta'en anither mate,
So we may mak our dinner sweet.

'Ye'll sit on his white hause-bane,
And I'll pike out his bonny blue e'en:
Wi' ae lock o' his gowden hair
We'll theek our nest when it grows bare.

'Mony a one for him maks mane,
But nane sall ken whar he is gane:
O'er his white banes, when they are bare,
The wind sall blaw for evermair.'

381. *A Lyke-Wake Dirge*

THIS ae nighte, this ae nighte,
    —*Every nighte and alle,*
Fire and fleet and candle-lighte,
    And Christe receive thy saule.

When thou from hence away art past,
    —*Every nighte and alle,*
To Whinny-muir thou com'st at last;
    And Christe receive thy saule.

If ever thou gavest hosen and shoon,
    —*Every nighte and alle,*
Sit thee down and put them on;
    And Christe receive thy saule.

If hosen and shoon thou ne'er gav'st nane
    —*Every nighte and alle,*

380. fail] turf.   hause] neck.   theek] thatch.
381. fleet] house-room.

124

The whinnes sall prick thee to the bare bane;
And Christe receive thy saule.

From Whinny-muir when thou may'st pass,
—*Every nighte and alle,*
To Brig o' Dread thou com'st at last;
And Christe receive thy saule.

From Brig o' Dread when thou may'st pass,
—*Every nighte and alle,*
To Purgatory fire thou com'st at last;
And Christe receive thy saule.

If ever thou gavest meat or drink,
—*Every nighte and alle,*
The fire sall never make thee shrink;
And Christe receive thy saule.

If meat or drink thou ne'er gav'st nane,
—*Every nighte and alle,*
The fire will burn thee to the bare bane;
And Christe receive thy saule.

This ae nighte, this ae nighte,
—*Every nighte and alle,*
Fire and sleet and candle-lighte,
And Christe receive thy saule.

382. *The Seven Virgins*

A Carol

ALL under the leaves and the leaves of life
I met with virgins seven,
And one of them was Mary mild,
Our Lord's mother of Heaven.

'O what are you seeking, you seven fair maids,
All under the leaves of life?
Come tell, come tell, what seek you
All under the leaves of life?'

'We're seeking for no leaves, Thomas,
    But for a friend of thine;
We're seeking for sweet Jesus Christ,
    To be our guide and thine.'

'Go down, go down, to yonder town,
    And sit in the gallery,
And there you'll see sweet Jesus Christ
    Nail'd to a big yew-tree.'

So down they went to yonder town
    As fast as foot could fall,
And many a grievous bitter tear
    From the virgins' eyes did fall.

'O peace, Mother, O peace, Mother,
    Your weeping doth me grieve:
I must suffer this,' He said,
    'For Adam and for Eve.

'O Mother, take you John Evangelist
    All for to be your son,
And he will comfort you sometimes,
    Mother, as I have done.'

'O come, thou John Evangelist,
    Thou'rt welcome unto me;
But more welcome my own dear Son,
    Whom I nursed on my knee.'

Then He laid His head on His right shoulder,
    Seeing death it struck Him nigh—
'The Holy Ghost be with your soul,
    I die, Mother dear, I die.'

O the rose, the gentle rose,
    And the fennel that grows so green!
God give us grace in every place
    To pray for our king and queen.

Furthermore for our enemies all
    Our prayers they should be strong:
Amen, good Lord; your charity
    Is the ending of my song.

383.   *Two Rivers*

S AYS Tweed to Till—
    'What gars ye rin sae still?'
Says Till to Tweed—
'Though ye rin with speed
    And I rin slaw,
For ae man that ye droon
    I droon twa.'

384.   *Cradle Song*

O M Y deir hert, young Jesus sweit,
    Prepare thy creddil in my spreit,
And I sall rock thee in my hert
And never mair from thee depart.

But I sall praise thee evermoir
With sangis sweit unto thy gloir;
The knees of my hert sall I bow,
And sing that richt *Balulalow!*

385.   *The Call*

M Y blood so red
    For thee was shed,
Come home again, come home again;
My own sweet heart, come home again!
    You've gone astray
    Out of your way,
Come home again, come home again!

386. *The Bonny Earl of Murray*

YE Highlands and ye Lawlands,
    O where hae ye been?
They hae slain the Earl of Murray,
    And hae laid him on the green.

Now wae be to thee, Huntley!
    And whairfore did ye sae!
I bade you bring him wi' you,
    But forbade you him to slay.

He was a braw gallant,
    And he rid at the ring;
And the bonny Earl of Murray,
    O he might hae been a king!

He was a braw gallant,
    And he play'd at the ba';
And the bonny Earl of Murray
    Was the flower amang them a'!

He was a braw gallant,
    And he play'd at the gluve;
And the bonny Earl of Murray,
    O he was the Queen's luve!

O lang will his Lady
    Look owre the Castle Downe,
Ere she see the Earl of Murray
    Come sounding through the town!

387. *Helen of Kirconnell*

I WISH I were where Helen lies,
    Night and day on me she cries;
O that I were where Helen lies,
    On fair Kirconnell lea!

Curst be the heart that thought the thought,
And curst the hand that fired the shot,
When in my arms burd Helen dropt,
    And died to succour me!

O think na ye my heart was sair,
When my Love dropp'd and spak nae mair!
There did she swoon wi' meikle care,
    On fair Kirconnell lea.

As I went down the water side,
None but my foe to be my guide,
None but my foe to be my guide,
    On fair Kirconnell lea;

I lighted down my sword to draw,
I hackéd him in pieces sma',
I hackéd him in pieces sma',
    For her sake that died for me.

O Helen fair, beyond compare!
I'll mak a garland o' thy hair,
Shall bind my heart for evermair,
    Until the day I die!

O that I were where Helen lies!
Night and day on me she cries;
Out of my bed she bids me rise,
    Says, 'Haste, and come to me!'

O Helen fair! O Helen chaste!
If I were with thee, I'd be blest,
Where thou lies low and taks thy rest,
    On fair Kirconnell lea.

I wish my grave were growing green,
A winding-sheet drawn owre my e'en,
And I in Helen's arms lying,
    On fair Kirconnell lea.

I wish I were where Helen lies!
Night and day on me she cries;
And I am weary of the skies,
    For her sake that died for me.

388.   *Waly, Waly*

O WALY, waly, up the bank,
    And waly, waly, doun the brae,
And waly, waly, yon burn-side,
    Where I and my Love wont to gae!
I lean'd my back unto an aik,
    I thocht it was a trustie tree;
But first it bow'd and syne it brak—
    Sae my true love did lichtlie me.

O waly, waly, gin love be bonnie
    A little time while it is new!
But when 'tis auld it waxeth cauld,
    And fades awa' like morning dew.
O wherefore should I busk my heid,
    Or wherefore should I kame my hair?
For my true Love has me forsook,
    And says he'll never lo'e me mair.

Now Arthur's Seat sall be my bed,
    The sheets sall ne'er be 'filed by me;
Saint Anton's well sall be my drink;
    Since my true Love has forsaken me.
Marti'mas wind, when wilt thou blaw,
    And shake the green leaves aff the tree?
O gentle Death, when wilt thou come?
    For of my life I am wearíe.

'Tis not the frost, that freezes fell,
    Nor blawing snaw's inclemencie,
'Tis not sic cauld that makes me cry;
    But my Love's heart grown cauld to me.

When we cam in by Glasgow toun,
    We were a comely sicht to see;
My Love was clad in the black velvét,
    And I mysel in cramasie.

But had I wist, before I kist,
    That love had been sae ill to win,
I had lock'd my heart in a case o' gowd,
    And pinn'd it wi' a siller pin.
And O! if my young babe were born,
    And set upon the nurse's knee;
And I mysel were dead and gane,
    And the green grass growing over me!

389.   *Barbara Allen's Cruelty*

IN Scarlet town, where I was born,
    There was a fair maid dwellin',
Made every youth cry *Well-a-way!*
    Her name was Barbara Allen.

All in the merry month of May,
    When green buds they were swellin',
Young Jemmy Grove on his death-bed lay,
    For love of Barbara Allen.

He sent his man in to her then,
    To the town where she was dwellin',
'O haste and come to my master dear,
    If your name be Barbara Allen.'

So slowly, slowly rase she up,
    And slowly she came nigh him,
And when she drew the curtain by—
    'Young man, I think you're dyin'.'

388. cramasie] crimson.

'O it 's I am sick and very very sick,
  And it 's all for Barbara Allen.'
'O the better for me ye'se never be,
  Tho' your heart's blood were a-spillin'!

'O dinna ye mind, young man,' says she,
  'When the red wine ye were fillin',
That ye made the healths go round and round,
  And slighted Barbara Allen?'

He turn'd his face unto the wall,
  And death was with him dealin':
'Adieu, adieu, my dear friends all,
  And be kind to Barbara Allen!'

As she was walking o'er the fields,
  She heard the dead-bell knellin';
And every jow the dead-bell gave
  Cried 'Woe to Barbara Allen.'

'O mother, mother, make my bed,
  O make it saft and narrow:
My love has died for me to-day,
  I'll die for him to-morrow.

'Farewell,' she said, 'ye virgins all,
  And shun the fault I fell in:
Henceforth take warning by the fall
  Of cruel Barbara Allen.'

390.   *Pipe and Can*

I

THE Indian weed witheréd quite;
 Green at morn, cut down at night;
Shows thy decay: all flesh is hay:
  Thus think, then drink Tobacco.

389. jow] beat, toll.

And when the smoke ascends on high,
Think thou behold'st the vanity
Of worldly stuff, gone with a puff:
      Thus think, then drink Tobacco.

But when the pipe grows foul within,
Think of thy soul defiled with sin,
And that the fire doth it require:
      Thus think, then drink Tobacco.

The ashes, that are left behind,
May serve to put thee still in mind
That unto dust return thou must:
      Thus think, then drink Tobacco.

II

WHEN as the chill Charokko blows,
    And Winter tells a heavy tale;
When pyes and daws and rooks and crows
Sit cursing of the frosts and snows;
    Then give me ale.

Ale in a Saxon rumkin then,
Such as will make grimalkin prate;
Bids valour burgeon in tall men,
Quickens the poet's wit and pen,
    Despises fate.

Ale, that the absent battle fights,
And frames the march of Swedish drum,
Disputes with princes, laws, and rights,
What 's done and past tells mortal wights,
    And what 's to come.

Charokko] Scirocco.

Ale, that the plowman's heart up-keeps
And equals it with tyrants' thrones,
That wipes the eye that over-weeps,
And lulls in sure and dainty sleeps
   Th' o'er-wearied bones.

Grandchild of Ceres, Bacchus' daughter,
Wine's emulous neighbour, though but stale,
Ennobling all the nymphs of water,
And filling each man's heart with laughter—
   Ha! give me ale!

391. *Love Will Find Out the Way*

OVER the mountains
  And over the waves,
Under the fountains
  And under the graves;
Under floods that are deepest,
  Which Neptune obey,
Over rocks that are steepest,
  Love will find out the way.

When there is no place
  For the glow-worm to lie,
When there is no space
  For receipt of a fly;
When the midge dares not venture
  Lest herself fast she lay,
If Love come, he will enter
  And will find out the way.

You may esteem him
  A child for his might;
Or you may deem him
  A coward for his flight;

ANONYMOUS

But if she whom Love doth honour
        Be conceal'd from the day—
Set a thousand guards upon her,
        Love will find out the way.

Some think to lose him
        By having him confined;
And some do suppose him,
        Poor heart! to be blind;
But if ne'er so close ye wall him,
        Do the best that ye may,
Blind Love, if so ye call him,
        He will find out his way.

You may train the eagle
        To stoop to your fist;
Or you may inveigle
        The Phoenix of the east;
The lioness, you may move her
        To give over her prey;
But you'll ne'er stop a lover—
        He will find out the way.

If the earth it should part him,
        He would gallop it o'er;
If the seas should o'erthwart him,
        He would swim to the shore;
Should his Love become a swallow,
        Through the air to stray,
Love will lend wings to follow,
        And will find out the way.

There is no striving
        To cross his intent;
There is no contriving
        His plots to prevent;

But if once the message greet him
  That his True Love doth stay,
If Death should come and meet him,
  Love will find out the way!

392. *Phillada Flouts Me*

O WHAT a plague is love!
    How shall I bear it?
She will inconstant prove,
    I greatly fear it.
She so torments my mind
    That my strength faileth,
And wavers with the wind
    As a ship saileth.
Please her the best I may,
She loves still to gainsay;
Alack and well-a-day!
    Phillada flouts me.

At the fair yesterday
    She did pass by me;
She look'd another way
    And would not spy me:
I woo'd her for to dine,
    But could not get her;
Will had her to the wine—
    He might entreat her.
With Daniel she did dance,
On me she look'd askance:
O thrice unhappy chance!
    Phillada flouts me.

Fair maid, be not so coy,
    Do not disdain me!
I am my mother's joy:
    Sweet, entertain me!

She'll give me, when she dies,
    All that is fitting:
Her poultry and her bees,
    And her goose sitting,
A pair of mattrass beds,
And a bag full of shreds;
And yet, for all this guedes,
    Phillada flouts me!

She hath a clout of mine
    Wrought with blue coventry,
Which she keeps for a sign
    Of my fidelity:
But i' faith, if she flinch
    She shall not wear it;
To Tib, my t'other wench,
    I mean to bear it.
And yet it grieves my heart
So soon from her to part:
Death strike me with his dart!
    Phillada flouts me.

Thou shalt eat crudded cream
    All the year lasting,
And drink the crystal stream
    Pleasant in tasting;
Whig and whey whilst thou lust,
    And bramble-berries,
Pie-lid and pastry-crust,
    Pears, plums, and cherries.
Thy raiment shall be thin,
Made of a weevil's skin—
Yet all 's not worth a pin!
    Phillada flouts me.

guedes] goods, property of any kind.

ANONYMOUS

In the last month of May
    I made her posies;
I heard her often say
    That she loved roses.
Cowslips and gillyflowers
    And the white lily
I brought to deck the bowers
    For my sweet Philly.
But she did all disdain,
And threw them back again;
Therefore 'tis flat and plain
    Phillada flouts me.

Fair maiden, have a care,
    And in time take me;
I can have those as fair
    If you forsake me:
For Doll the dairy-maid
    Laugh'd at me lately,
And wanton Winifred
    Favours me greatly.
One throws milk on my clothes,
T'other plays with my nose;
What wanting signs are those?
    Phillada flouts me.

I cannot work nor sleep
    At all in season:
Love wounds my heart so deep
    Without all reason.
I 'gin to pine away
    In my love's shadow,
Like as a fat beast may,
    Penn'd in a meadow.

I shall be dead, I fear,
   Within this thousand year:
And all for that my dear
   Phillada flouts me.

WILLIAM STRODE

1602–1645

393.   *Chloris in the Snow*

I SAW fair Chloris walk alone,
   When feather'd rain came softly down,
As Jove descending from his Tower
To court her in a silver shower:
The wanton snow flew to her breast,
Like pretty birds into their nest,
But, overcome with whiteness there,
For grief it thaw'd into a tear:
   Thence falling on her garments' hem,
   To deck her, froze into a gem.

THOMAS STANLEY

1625–1678

394.   *The Relapse*

O TURN away those cruel eyes,
   The stars of my undoing!
Or death, in such a bright disguise,
   May tempt a second wooing.

Punish their blind and impious pride,
   Who dare contemn thy glory;
It was my fall that deified
   Thy name, and seal'd thy story.

Yet no new sufferings can prepare
 A higher praise to crown thee;
Though my first death proclaim thee fair,
 My second will unthrone thee.

Lovers will doubt thou canst entice
 No other for thy fuel,
And if thou burn one victim twice,
 Both think thee poor and cruel.

THOMAS D'URFEY

1653–1723

395.   *Chloe Divine*

CHLOE 's a Nymph in flowery groves,
 A Nereid in the streams;
Saint-like she in the temple moves,
 A woman in my dreams.

Love steals artillery from her eyes,
 The Graces point her charms;
Orpheus is rivall'd in her voice,
 And Venus in her arms.

Never so happily in one
 Did heaven and earth combine:
And yet 'tis flesh and blood alone
 That makes her so divine.

CHARLES COTTON

1630–1687

396.   *To Cœlia*

WHEN, Cœlia, must my old day set,
        And my young morning rise
In beams of joy so bright as yet
        Ne'er bless'd a lover's eyes?
My state is more advanced than when
        I first attempted thee:
I sued to be a servant then,
        But now to be made free.

I've served my time faithful and true,
        Expecting to be placed
In happy freedom, as my due,
        To all the joys thou hast:
Ill husbandry in love is such
        A scandal to love's power,
We ought not to misspend so much
        As one poor short-lived hour.

Yet think not, sweet, I'm weary grown,
        That I pretend such haste;
Since none to surfeit e'er was known
        Before he had a taste:
My infant love could humbly wait
        When, young, it scarce knew how
To plead; but grown to man's estate,
        He is impatient now.

KATHERINE PHILIPS ('ORINDA')

1631–1664

397. To One Persuading a Lady to Marriage

FORBEAR, bold youth; all 's heaven here,
 And what you do aver
To others courtship may appear,
 'Tis sacrilege to her.
She is a public deity;
 And were 't not very odd
She should dispose herself to be
 A petty household god?

First make the sun in private shine
 And bid the world adieu,
That so he may his beams confine
 In compliment to you:
But if of that you do despair,
 Think how you did amiss
To strive to fix her beams which are
 More bright and large than his.

JOHN DRYDEN

1631–1700

398. Ode

To the Pious Memory of the Accomplished Young Lady, Mrs. Anne Killigrew, excellent in the Two Sister Arts of Poesy and Painting

THOU youngest virgin-daughter of the skies,
 Made in the last promotion of the blest;
Whose palms, new pluck'd from Paradise,
In spreading branches more sublimely rise,

Rich with immortal green above the rest:
Whether, adopted to some neighbouring star,
Thou roll'st above us, in thy wandering race,
    Or, in procession fixt and regular,
    Mov'd with the heaven's majestic pace;
    Or, call'd to more superior bliss,
Thou tread'st with seraphims the vast abyss:
Whatever happy region is thy place,
Cease thy celestial song a little space;
Thou wilt have time enough for hymns divine,
    Since Heaven's eternal year is thine.
Hear, then, a mortal Muse thy praise rehearse,
      In no ignoble verse;
But such as thy own voice did practise here,
When thy first-fruits of Poesy were given,
To make thyself a welcome inmate there;
    While yet a young probationer,
      And candidate of heaven.

    If by traduction came thy mind,
    Our wonder is the less, to find
A soul so charming from a stock so good;
Thy father was transfus'd into thy blood:
So wert thou born into the tuneful strain,
An early, rich, and inexhausted vein.
    But if thy pre-existing soul
    Was form'd at first with myriads more,
It did through all the mighty poets roll
    Who Greek or Latin laurels wore,
And was that Sappho last, which once it was before.
    If so, then cease thy flight, O heaven-born mind!
Thou hast no dross to purge from thy rich ore:
    Nor can thy soul a fairer mansion find,
    Than was the beauteous frame she left behind:
Return, to fill or mend the quire of thy celestial kind.

May we presume to say, that, at thy birth,
New joy was sprung in heaven as well as here on earth?
    For sure the milder planets did combine
    On thy auspicious horoscope to shine,
    And even the most malicious were in trine.
        Thy brother-angels at thy birth
        Strung each his lyre, and tun'd it high,
        That all the people of the sky
    Might know a poetess was born on earth;
        And then, if ever, mortal ears
        Had heard the music of the spheres.
        And if no clust'ring swarm of bees
    On thy sweet mouth distill'd their golden dew,
        'Twas that such vulgar miraclés
        Heaven had not leisure to renew:
    For all the blest fraternity of love
Solemniz'd there thy birth, and kept thy holiday above.

    O gracious God! how far have we
Profaned thy heavenly gift of Poesy!
Made prostitute and profligate the Muse,
Debas'd to each obscene and impious use,
Whose harmony was first ordain'd above,
For tongues of angels and for hymns of love!
O wretched we! why were we hurried down
    This lubrique and adulterate age
(Nay, added fat pollutions of our own),
    To increase the streaming ordures of the stage?
What can we say to excuse our second fall?
Let this thy Vestal, Heaven, atone for all!
Her Arethusian stream remains unsoil'd,
    Unmixt with foreign filth, and undefil'd;
Her wit was more than man, her innocence a child.

Art she had none, yet wanted none,
    For Nature did that want supply:
So rich in treasures of her own,
    She might our boasted stores defy:
Such noble vigour did her verse adorn,
That it seem'd borrow'd, where 'twas only born.
Her morals, too, were in her bosom bred,
    By great examples daily fed,
What in the best of books, her father's life, she read.
    And to be read herself she need not fear;
Each test, and every light, her Muse will bear,
Though Epictetus with his lamp were there.
Even love (for love sometimes her Muse exprest)
Was but a lambent flame which play'd about her breast,
    Light as the vapours of a morning dream;
So cold herself, whilst she such warmth exprest,
    'Twas Cupid bathing in Diana's stream. . . .

    Now all those charms, that blooming grace,
The well-proportion'd shape, and beauteous face,
Shall never more be seen by mortal eyes;
In earth the much-lamented virgin lies.
Not wit, nor piety could fate prevent;
Nor was the cruel destiny content
To finish all the murder at a blow,
To sweep at once her life and beauty too;
But, like a harden'd felon, took a pride
    To work more mischievously slow,
    And plunder'd first, and then destroy'd.
O double sacrilege on things divine,
To rob the relic, and deface the shrine!
      But thus Orinda died:
Heaven, by the same disease, did both translate;
As equal were their souls, so equal was their fate.

Meantime, her warlike brother on the seas
His waving streamers to the winds displays,
And vows for his return, with vain devotion, pays.
    Ah, generous youth! that wish forbear,
    The winds too soon will waft thee here!
    Slack all thy sails, and fear to come,
Alas, thou know'st not, thou art wreck'd at home!
No more shalt thou behold thy sister's face,
Thou hast already had her last embrace.
But look aloft, and if thou kenn'st from far,
Among the Pleiads a new kindl'd star,
If any sparkles than the rest more bright,
'Tis she that shines in that propitious light.

When in mid-air the golden trump shall sound,
    To raise the nations under ground;
When, in the Valley of Jehoshaphat,
The judging God shall close the book of Fate,
    And there the last assizes keep
    For those who wake and those who sleep;
    When rattling bones together fly
    From the four corners of the sky;
When sinews o'er the skeletons are spread,
Those cloth'd with flesh, and life inspires the dead;
The sacred poets first shall hear the sound,
    And foremost from the tomb shall bound,
For they are cover'd with the lightest ground;
And straight, with inborn vigour, on the wing,
Like mounting larks, to the new morning sing.
There thou, sweet Saint, before the quire shalt go,
As harbinger of Heaven, the way to show,
The way which thou so well hast learn'd below.

399. *A Song for St. Cecilia's Day, 1687*

FROM harmony, from heavenly harmony,
    This universal frame began:
  When nature underneath a heap
    Of jarring atoms lay,
    And could not heave her head,
The tuneful voice was heard from high,
    'Arise, ye more than dead!'
Then cold, and hot, and moist, and dry,
    In order to their stations leap,
      And Music's power obey.
From harmony, from heavenly harmony,
    This universal frame began:
    From harmony to harmony
Through all the compass of the notes it ran,
The diapason closing full in Man.

What passion cannot Music raise and quell?
    When Jubal struck the chorded shell,
  His listening brethren stood around,
    And, wondering, on their faces fell
To worship that celestial sound:
Less than a God they thought there could not dwell
    Within the hollow of that shell,
    That spoke so sweetly, and so well.
What passion cannot Music raise and quell?

    The trumpet's loud clangour
      Excites us to arms,
   With shrill notes of anger,
    And mortal alarms.
The double double double beat
    Of the thundering drum
   Cries Hark! the foes come;
Charge, charge, 'tis too late to retreat!

The soft complaining flute,
In dying notes, discovers
The woes of hopeless lovers,
Whose dirge is whisper'd by the warbling lute.

Sharp violins proclaim
Their jealous pangs and desperation,
Fury, frantic indignation,
Depth of pains, and height of passion,
For the fair, disdainful dame.

But O, what art can teach,
What human voice can reach,
The sacred organ's praise?
Notes inspiring holy love,
Notes that wing their heavenly ways
To mend the choirs above.

Orpheus could lead the savage race;
And trees unrooted left their place,
Sequacious of the lyre;
But bright Cecilia rais'd the wonder higher:
When to her organ vocal breath was given,
An angel heard, and straight appear'd
Mistaking Earth for Heaven.

Grand Chorus
As from the power of sacred lays
The spheres began to move,
And sung the great Creator's praise
To all the Blest above;
So when the last and dreadful hour
This crumbling pageant shall devour,
The trumpet shall be heard on high,
The dead shall live, the living die,
And Music shall untune the sky!

400.   *Ah, How Sweet It Is to Love!*

AH, how sweet it is to love!
  Ah, how gay is young Desire!
And what pleasing pains we prove
  When we first approach Love's fire!
Pains of love be sweeter far
Than all other pleasures are.

Sighs which are from lovers blown
  Do but gently heave the heart:
Ev'n the tears they shed alone
  Cure, like trickling balm, their smart:
Lovers, when they lose their breath,
Bleed away in easy death.

Love and Time with reverence use,
  Treat them like a parting friend;
Nor the golden gifts refuse
  Which in youth sincere they send:
For each year their price is more,
And they less simple than before.

Love, like spring-tides full and high,
  Swells in every youthful vein;
But each tide does less supply,
  Till they quite shrink in again:
If a flow in age appear,
'Tis but rain, and runs not clear.

401. *Hidden Flame*

I FEED a flame within, which so torments me
  That it both pains my heart, and yet contents me:
'Tis such a pleasing smart, and I so love it,
That I had rather die than once remove it.

Yet he, for whom I grieve, shall never know it;
My tongue does not betray, nor my eyes show it.
Not a sigh, nor a tear, my pain discloses,
But they fall silently, like dew on roses.

Thus, to prevent my Love from being cruel,
My heart 's the sacrifice, as 'tis the fuel;
And while I suffer this to give him quiet,
My faith rewards my love, though he deny it.

On his eyes will I gaze, and there delight me;
While I conceal my love no frown can fright me.
To be more happy I dare not aspire,
Nor can I fall more low, mounting no higher.

402. *Song to a Fair Young Lady, Going out of the Town in the Spring*

ASK not the cause why sullen Spring
  So long delays her flowers to bear;
Why warbling birds forget to sing,
  And winter storms invert the year:
Chloris is gone; and fate provides
To make it Spring where she resides.

Chloris is gone, the cruel fair;
  She cast not back a pitying eye:
But left her lover in despair
  To sigh, to languish, and to die:
Ah! how can those fair eyes endure
To give the wounds they will not cure?

Great God of Love, why hast thou made
   A face that can all hearts command,
That all religions can invade,
   And change the laws of every land?
Where thou hadst placed such power before,
     Thou shouldst have made her mercy more.

When Chloris to the temple comes,
   Adoring crowds before her fall;
She can restore the dead from tombs
   And every life but mine recall.
I only am by Love design'd
To be the victim for mankind.

CHARLES WEBBE

c.1678

403.   *Against Indifference*

MORE love or more disdain I crave;
   Sweet, be not still indifferent:
O send me quickly to my grave,
   Or else afford me more content!
Or love or hate me more or less,
For love abhors all lukewarmness.

Give me a tempest if 'twill drive
   Me to the place where I would be;
Or if you'll have me still alive,
   Confess you will be kind to me.
Give hopes of bliss or dig my grave:
More love or more disdain I crave.

SIR GEORGE ETHEREGE

1635–1691

404.   *Song*

LADIES, though to your conquering eyes
    Love owes his chiefest victories,
And borrows those bright arms from you
With which he does the world subdue,
Yet you yourselves are not above
The empire nor the griefs of love.

Then rack not lovers with disdain,
Lest Love on you revenge their pain:
You are not free because you're fair:
The Boy did not his Mother spare.
Beauty 's but an offensive dart:
It is no armour for the heart.

405. ***To a Lady Asking Him How
Long He Would Love Her***

IT is not, Celia, in our power
    To say how long our love will last;
It may be we within this hour
    May lose those joys we now do taste;
The Bléssed, that immortal be,
From change in love are only free.

Then since we mortal lovers are,
    Ask not how long our love will last;
But while it does, let us take care
    Each minute be with pleasure past:
Were it not madness to deny
To live because we're sure to die?

THOMAS TRAHERNE

1637?–1674

406.   *News*

NEWS from a foreign country came
As if my treasure and my wealth lay there;
So much it did my heart inflame,
'Twas wont to call my Soul into mine ear;
Which thither went to meet
The approaching sweet,
And on the threshold stood
To entertain the unknown Good.
It hover'd there
As if 'twould leave mine ear,
And was so eager to embrace
The joyful tidings as they came,
'Twould almost leave its dwelling-place
To entertain that same.

As if the tidings were the things,
My very joys themselves, my foreign treasure—
Or else did bear them on their wings—
With so much joy they came, with so much pleasure.
My Soul stood at that gate
To recreate
Itself with bliss, and to
Be pleased with speed. A fuller view
It fain would take,
Yet journeys back would make
Unto my heart; as if 'twould fain
Go out to meet, yet stay within
To fit a place to entertain
And bring the tidings in.

What sacred instinct did inspire
My soul in childhood with a hope so strong?

What secret force moved my desire
To expect my joys beyond the seas, so young?
Felicity I knew
Was out of view,
And being here alone,
I saw that happiness was gone
From me! For this
I thirsted absent bliss,
And thought that sure beyond the seas,
Or else in something near at hand—
I knew not yet—since naught did please
I knew—my Bliss did stand.

But little did the infant dream
That all the treasures of the world were by:
And that himself was so the cream
And crown of all which round about did lie.
Yet thus it was: the Gem,
The Diadem,
The ring enclosing all
That stood upon this earthly ball,
The Heavenly eye,
Much wider than the sky,
Wherein they all included were,
The glorious Soul, that was the King
Made to possess them, did appear
A small and little thing!

THOMAS FLATMAN

1637–1688

407.   *The Sad Day*

O THE sad day!
       When friends shall shake their heads, and say
Of miserable me—
'Hark, how he groans!
Look, how he pants for breath!
See how he struggles with the pangs of death!'
When they shall say of these dear eyes—
'How hollow, O how dim they be!
Mark how his breast doth rise and swell
Against his potent enemy!'
When some old friend shall step to my bedside,
Touch my chill face, and thence shall gently slide.

But—when his next companions say
'How does he do? What hopes?'—shall turn away,
Answering only, with a lift-up hand—
'Who can his fate withstand?'

Then shall a gasp or two do more
Than e'er my rhetoric could before:
Persuade the world to trouble me no more!

CHARLES SACKVILLE, EARL OF DORSET

1638–1706

408.   *Song*

***Written at Sea, in the First Dutch War
(1665), the Night before an Engagement***

TO all you ladies now at land
     We men at sea indite;
But first would have you understand
     How hard it is to write:
The Muses now, and Neptune too,
We must implore to write to you—
         With a fa, la, la, la, la.

For though the Muses should prove kind,
     And fill our empty brain,
Yet if rough Neptune rouse the wind
     To wave the azure main,
Our paper, pen, and ink, and we,
Roll up and down our ships at sea—
         With a fa, la, la, la, la.

Then if we write not by each post,
     Think not we are unkind;
Nor yet conclude our ships are lost
     By Dutchmen or by wind:
Our tears we'll send a speedier way,
The tide shall bring them twice a day—
         With a fa, la, la, la, la.

The King with wonder and surprise
     Will swear the seas grow bold,
Because the tides will higher rise
     Than e'er they did of old:

But let him know it is our tears
Bring floods of grief to Whitehall stairs—
    With a fa, la, la, la, la.

Should foggy Opdam chance to know
    Our sad and dismal story,
The Dutch would scorn so weak a foe,
    And quit their fort at Goree:
For what resistance can they find
From men who've left their hearts behind?—
    With a fa, la, la, la, la.

Let wind and weather do its worst,
    Be you to us but kind;
Let Dutchmen vapour, Spaniards curse,
    No sorrow we shall find:
'Tis then no matter how things go,
Or who's our friend, or who's our foe—
    With a fa, la, la, la, la.

To pass our tedious hours away
    We throw a merry main,
Or else at serious ombre play;
    But why should we in vain
Each other's ruin thus pursue?
We were undone when we left you—
    With a fa, la, la, la, la.

But now our fears tempestuous grow
    And cast our hopes away;
Whilst you, regardless of our woe,
    Sit careless at a play:
Perhaps permit some happier man
To kiss your hand, or flirt your fan—
    With a fa, la, la, la, la..

When any mournful tune you hear,
    That dies in every note

As if it sigh'd with each man's care
    For being so remote,
Think then how often love we've made
To you, when all those tunes were play'd—
    With a fa, la, la, la, la.

In justice you cannot refuse
    To think of our distress,
When we for hopes of honour lose
    Our certain happiness:
All those designs are but to prove
Ourselves more worthy of your love—
    With a fa, la, la, la, la.

And now we've told you all our loves,
    And likewise all our fears,
In hopes this declaration moves
    Some pity for our tears:
Let's hear of no inconstancy—
We have too much of that at sea—
    With a fa, la, la, la, la.

SIR CHARLES SEDLEY

1639–1701

409.   *To Chloris*

AH, Chloris! that I now could sit
    As unconcern'd as when
Your infant beauty could beget
    No pleasure, nor no pain!
When I the dawn used to admire,
    And praised the coming day,
I little thought the growing fire
    Must take my rest away.

Your charms in harmless childhood lay
    Like metals in the mine;

Age from no face took more away
    Than youth conceal'd in thine.
But as your charms insensibly
    To their perfection prest,
Fond love as unperceived did fly,
    And in my bosom rest.

My passion with your beauty grew,
    And Cupid at my heart,
Still as his mother favour'd you,
    Threw a new flaming dart:
Each gloried in their wanton part;
    To make a lover, he
Employ'd the utmost of his art—
    To make a beauty, she.

410. *To Celia*

NOT, Celia, that I juster am
    Or better than the rest!
For I would change each hour, like them,
    Were not my heart at rest.

But I am tied to very thee
    By every thought I have;
Thy face I only care to see,
    Thy heart I only crave.

All that in woman is adored
    In thy dear self I find—
For the whole sex can but afford
    The handsome and the kind.

Why then should I seek further store,
    And still make love anew?
When change itself can give no more,
    'Tis easy to be true!

APHRA BEHN

1640–1689

411.   *Song*

L OVE in fantastic triumph sate
    Whilst bleeding hearts around him flow'd,
For whom fresh pains he did create
    And strange tyrannic power he show'd:
From thy bright eyes he took his fires,
    Which round about in sport he hurl'd;
But 'twas from mine he took desires
    Enough t' undo the amorous world.

From me he took his sighs and tears,
    From thee his pride and cruelty;
From me his languishments and fears,
    And every killing dart from thee.
Thus thou and I the god have arm'd
    And set him up a deity;
But my poor heart alone is harm'd,
    Whilst thine the victor is, and free!

412.   *The Libertine*

A THOUSAND martyrs I have made,
    All sacrificed to my desire,
A thousand beauties have betray'd
    That languish in resistless fire:
The untamed heart to hand I brought,
    And fix'd the wild and wand'ring thought.

I never vow'd nor sigh'd in vain,
    But both, tho' false, were well received;
The fair are pleased to give us pain,
    And what they wish is soon believed:

And tho' I talk'd of wounds and smart,
    Love's pleasures only touch'd my heart.

Alone the glory and the spoil
    I always laughing bore away;
The triumphs without pain or toil,
    Without the hell the heaven of joy;
And while I thus at random rove
    Despise the fools that whine for love.

JOHN WILMOT, EARL OF ROCHESTER

1647–1680

413.   *Return*

ABSENT from thee, I languish still;
    Then ask me not, When I return?
The straying fool 'twill plainly kill
    To wish all day, all night to mourn.

Dear, from thine arms then let me fly,
    That my fantastic mind may prove
The torments it deserves to try,
    That tears my fix'd heart from my love.

When, wearied with a world of woe,
    To thy safe bosom I retire,
Where love, and peace, and truth does flow,
    May I contented there expire!

Lest, once more wandering from that heaven,
    I fall on some base heart unblest;
Faithless to thee, false, unforgiven—
    And lose my everlasting rest.

414. *Love and Life*

ALL my past life is mine no more;
　　The flying hours are gone,
Like transitory dreams given o'er,
Whose images are kept in store
　　By memory alone.

The time that is to come is not;
　　How can it then be mine?
The present moment 's all my lot;
And that, as fast as it is got,
　　Phillis, is only thine.

Then talk not of inconstancy,
　　False hearts, and broken vows;
If I by miracle can be
This live-long minute true to thee,
　　'Tis all that Heaven allows.

415. *Constancy*

I CANNOT change as others do,
　　Though you unjustly scorn;
Since that poor swain that sighs for you
　　For you alone was born.
No, Phillis, no; your heart to move
　　A surer way I'll try;
And, to revenge my slighted love,
　　Will still love on and die.

When kill'd with grief Amyntas lies,
　　And you to mind shall call
The sighs that now unpitied rise,
　　The tears that vainly fall—
That welcome hour, that ends this smart,
　　Will then begin your pain;
For such a faithful tender heart
　　Can never break in vain.

416. *To His Mistress*

(After Quarles)

WHY dost thou shade thy lovely face? O why
    Does that eclipsing hand of thine deny
The sunshine of the Sun's enlivening eye?

Without thy light what light remains in me?
Thou art my life; my way, my light 's in thee;
I live, I move, and by thy beams I see.

Thou art my life—if thou but turn away
My life 's a thousand deaths. Thou art my way—
Without thee, Love, I travel not but stray.

My light thou art—without thy glorious sight
My eyes are darken'd with eternal night.
My Love, thou art my way, my life, my light.

Thou art my way; I wander if thou fly.
Thou art my light; if hid, how blind am I!
Thou art my life; if thou withdraw'st, I die.

My eyes are dark and blind, I cannot see:
To whom or whither should my darkness flee,
But to that light?—and who 's that light but thee?

If I have lost my path, dear lover, say,
Shall I still wander in a doubtful way?
Love, shall a lamb of Israel's sheepfold stray?

My path is lost, my wandering steps do stray;
I cannot go, nor can I safely stay;
Whom should I seek but thee, my path, my way?

And yet thou turn'st thy face away and fly'st me!
And yet I sue for grace and thou deny'st me!
Speak, art thou angry, Love, or only try'st me?

Thou art the pilgrim's path, the blind man's eye,
The dead man's life. On thee my hopes rely:
If I but them remove, I surely die.

Dissolve thy sunbeams, close thy wings and stay!
See, see how I am blind, and dead, and stray!
—O thou that art my life, my light, my way!

Then work thy will! If passion bid me flee,
My reason shall obey, my wings shall be
Stretch'd out no farther than from me to thee!

JOHN SHEFFIELD, DUKE OF BUCKINGHAMSHIRE

1649–1720

417.   *The Reconcilement*

COME, let us now resolve at last
    To live and love in quiet;
We'll tie the knot so very fast
    That Time shall ne'er untie it.

The truest joys they seldom prove
    Who free from quarrels live:
'Tis the most tender part of love
    Each other to forgive.

When least I seem'd concern'd, I took
    No pleasure nor no rest;
And when I feign'd an angry look,
    Alas! I loved you best.

Own but the same to me—you'll find
    How blest will be our fate.
O to be happy—to be kind—
    Sure never is too late!

418. ***On One Who Died***
Discovering Her Kindness

SOME vex their souls with jealous pain,
 While others sigh for cold disdain:
Love's various slaves we daily see—
Yet happy all compared with me!

Of all mankind I loved the best
A nymph so far above the rest
That we outshined the Blest above;
In beauty she, as I in love.

And therefore They, who could not bear
To be outdone by mortals here,
Among themselves have placed her now,
And left me wretched here below.

All other fate I could have borne,
And even endured her very scorn;
But oh! thus all at once to find
That dread account—both dead and kind!
What heart can hold? If yet I live,
'Tis but to show how much I grieve.

THOMAS OTWAY

1652–1685

419. ***The Enchantment***

I DID but look and love awhile,
 'Twas but for one half-hour;
Then to resist I had no will,
 And now I have no power.

To sigh and wish is all my ease;
 Sighs which do heat impart
Enough to melt the coldest ice,
 Yet cannot warm your heart.

O would your pity give my heart
    One corner of your breast,
'Twould learn of yours the winning art,
    And quickly steal the rest.

JOHN OLDHAM

1653–1683

420.   *A Quiet Soul*

THY soul within such silent pomp did keep,
  As if humanity were lull'd asleep;
So gentle was thy pilgrimage beneath,
    Time's unheard feet scarce make less noise,
    Or the soft journey which a planet goes:
Life seem'd all calm as its last breath.
    A still tranquillity so hush'd thy breast,
      As if some Halcyon were its guest,
      And there had built her nest;
It hardly now enjoys a greater rest.

JOHN CUTTS, LORD CUTTS

1661–1707

421.   *Song*

ONLY tell her that I love:
  Leave the rest to her and Fate:
Some kind planet from above
May perhaps her pity move:
    Lovers on their stars must wait.—
Only tell her that I love!

Why, O why should I despair!
    Mercy 's pictured in her eye:
If she once vouchsafe to hear,
Welcome Hope and farewell Fear!
    She 's too good to let me die.—
Why, O why should I despair?

MATTHEW PRIOR

1664–1721

422.   *The Question to Lisetta*

WHAT nymph should I admire or trust,
But Chloe beauteous, Chloe just?
What nymph should I desire to see,
But her who leaves the plain for me?
To whom should I compose the lay,
But her who listens when I play?
To whom in song repeat my cares,
But her who in my sorrow shares?
For whom should I the garland make,
But her who joys the gift to take,
And boasts she wears it for my sake?
In love am I not fully blest?
Lisetta, prithee tell the rest.

Lisetta's Reply
Sure Chloe just, and Chloe fair,
Deserves to be your only care;
But, when you and she to-day
Far into the wood did stray,
And I happen'd to pass by,
Which way did you cast your eye?
But, when your cares to her you sing,
You dare not tell her whence they spring:
Does it not more afflict your heart,
That in those cares she bears a part?
When you the flowers for Chloe twine,
Why do you to her garland join
The meanest bud that falls from mine?
Simplest of swains! the world may see
Whom Chloe loves, and who loves me.

423. *To a Child of Quality*

Five Years Old, 1704 — The Author Then Forty

L ORDS, knights, and squires, the numerous band
  That wear the fair Miss Mary's fetters,
Were summoned by her high command
  To show their passions by their letters.

My pen amongst the rest I took,
  Lest those bright eyes, that cannot read,
Should dart their kindling fire, and look
  The power they have to be obey'd.

Nor quality, nor reputation,
  Forbid me yet my flame to tell;
Dear Five-years-old befriends my passion,
  And I may write till she can spell.

For, while she makes her silkworms beds
  With all the tender things I swear;
Whilst all the house my passion reads,
  In papers round her baby's hair;

She may receive and own my flame;
  For, though the strictest prudes should know it,
She'll pass for a most virtuous dame,
  And I for an unhappy poet.

Then too, alas! when she shall tear
  The rhymes some younger rival sends,
She'll give me leave to write, I fear,
  And we shall still continue friends.

For, as our different ages move,
  'Tis so ordain'd (would Fate but mend it!),
That I shall be past making love
  When she begins to comprehend it.

424. *Song*

THE merchant, to secure his treasure,
    Conveys it in a borrow'd name:
Euphelia serves to grace my measure;
    But Chloe is my real flame.

My softest verse, my darling lyre,
    Upon Euphelia's toilet lay;
When Chloe noted her desire
    That I should sing, that I should play.

My lyre I tune, my voice I raise;
    But with my numbers mix my sighs:
And while I sing Euphelia's praise,
    I fix my soul on Chloe's eyes.

Fair Chloe blush'd: Euphelia frown'd:
    I sung, and gazed: I play'd, and trembled:
And Venus to the Loves around
    Remark'd, how ill we all dissembled.

425. *On My Birthday, July 21*

I, MY dear, was born to-day—
    So all my jolly comrades say:
They bring me music, wreaths, and mirth,
And ask to celebrate my birth:
Little, alas! my comrades know
That I was born to pain and woe;
To thy denial, to thy scorn,
Better I had ne'er been born:
I wish to die, even whilst I say—
'I, my dear, was born to-day.'

I, my dear, was born to-day:
Shall I salute the rising ray,

Well-spring of all my joy and woe?
Clotilda, thou alone dost know.
Shall the wreath surround my hair?
Or shall the music please my ear?
Shall I my comrades' mirth receive,
And bless my birth, and wish to live?
Then let me see great Venus chase
Imperious anger from thy face;
Then let me hear thee smiling say—
'Thou, my dear, wert born to-day.'

426. *The Lady Who Offers Her Looking-Glass to Venus*

VENUS, take my votive glass:
   Since I am not what I was,
What from this day I shall be,
Venus, let me never see.

427. *A Letter*

To Lady Margaret Cavendish Holles-Harley, When a Child

MY noble, lovely, little Peggy,
   Let this my First Epistle beg ye,
At dawn of morn, and close of even,
To lift your heart and hands to Heaven.
In double duty say your prayer:
Our Father first, then *Notre Père*.

And, dearest child, along the day,
In every thing you do and say,
Obey and please my lord and lady,
So God shall love and angels aid ye.

If to these precepts you attend,
No second letter need I send,
And so I rest your constant friend.

428.   *For My Own Monument*

A S doctors give physic by way of prevention,
 Mat, alive and in health, of his tombstone took care;
For delays are unsafe, and his pious intention
  May haply be never fulfill'd by his heir.

Then take Mat's word for it, the sculptor is paid;
  That the figure is fine, pray believe your own eye;
Yet credit but lightly what more may be said,
  For we flatter ourselves, and teach marble to lie.

Yet counting as far as to fifty his years,
  His virtues and vices were as other men's are;
High hopes he conceived, and he smother'd great fears,
  In a life parti-colour'd, half pleasure, half care.

Nor to business a drudge, nor to faction a slave,
  He strove to make int'rest and freedom agree;
In public employments industrious and grave,
  And alone with his friends, Lord! how merry was he!

Now in equipage stately, now humbly on foot,
  Both fortunes he tried, but to neither would trust;
And whirl'd in the round as the wheel turn'd about,
  He found riches had wings, and knew man was but dust.

This verse, little polish'd, tho' mighty sincere,
  Sets neither his titles nor merit to view;
It says that his relics collected lie here,
  And no mortal yet knows too if this may be true.

Fierce robbers there are that infest the highway,
  So Mat may be kill'd, and his bones never found;
False witness at court, and fierce tempests at sea,
  So Mat may yet chance to be hang'd or be drown'd.

If his bones lie in earth, roll in sea, fly in air,
  To Fate we must yield, and the thing is the same;
And if passing thou giv'st him a smile or a tear,
  He cares not—yet, prithee, be kind to his fame.

WILLIAM WALSH

1663–1708

429. *Rivals*

OF all the torments, all the cares,
 With which our lives are curst;
Of all the plagues a lover bears,
 Sure rivals are the worst!
By partners in each other kind
 Afflictions easier grow;
In love alone we hate to find
 Companions of our woe.

Sylvia, for all the pangs you see
 Are labouring in my breast,
I beg not you would favour me,
 Would you but slight the rest!
How great soe'er your rigours are,
 With them alone I'll cope;
I can endure my own despair,
 But not another's hope.

LADY GRISEL BAILLIE

1665–1746

430. *Werena My Heart's Licht I Wad Dee*

THERE ance was a may, and she lo'ed na men;
 She biggit her bonnie bow'r doun in yon glen;
But now she cries, Dool and a well-a-day!
Come doun the green gait and come here away!

When bonnie young Johnnie cam owre the sea,
He said he saw naething sae lovely as me;
He hecht me baith rings and mony braw things—
And werena my heart's licht, I wad dee.

430. may] maid. biggit] built. gait] way, path.
hecht] promised.

172

He had a wee titty that lo'ed na me,
Because I was twice as bonnie as she;
She raised sic a pother 'twixt him and his mother
That werena my heart's licht, I wad dee.

The day it was set, and the bridal to be:
The wife took a dwam and lay doun to dee;
She maned and she graned out o' dolour and pain,
Till he vow'd he never wad see me again.

His kin was for ane of a higher degree,
Said—What had he do wi' the likes of me?
Appose I was bonnie, I wasna for Johnnie—
And werena my heart's licht, I wad dee.

They said I had neither cow nor calf,
Nor dribbles o' drink rins thro' the draff,
Nor pickles o' meal rins thro' the mill-e'e—
And werena my heart's licht, I wad dee.

His titty she was baith wylie and slee:
She spied me as I cam owre the lea;
And then she ran in and made a loud din—
Believe your ain e'en, an ye trow not me.

His bonnet stood ay fu' round on his brow,
His auld ane look'd ay as well as some's new:
But now he lets 't wear ony gait it will hing,
And casts himsel dowie upon the corn bing.

And now he gaes daund'ring about the dykes,
And a' he dow do is to hund the tykes:
The live-lang nicht he ne'er steeks his e'e—
And werena my heart's licht, I wad dee.

titty] sister.   dwam] sudden illness.
appose] suppose.   pickles] small quantities.
hing] hang.   dowie] dejectedly.
hund the tykes] direct the dogs.   steeks] closes.

173

Were I but young for thee, as I hae been,
We should hae been gallopin' doun in yon green,
And linkin' it owre the lily-white lea—
And wow, gin I were but young for thee!

WILLIAM CONGREVE

1670–1729

431. *False Though She Be*

FALSE though she be to me and love,
    I'll ne'er pursue revenge;
For still the charmer I approve,
    Though I deplore her change.

In hours of bliss we oft have met:
    They could not always last;
And though the present I regret,
    I'm grateful for the past.

432. *A Hue and Cry after Fair Amoret*

FAIR Amoret is gone astray—
    Pursue and seek her, ev'ry lover;
I'll tell the signs by which you may
    The wand'ring Shepherdess discover.

Coquette and coy at once her air,
    Both studied, tho' both seem neglected;
Careless she is, with artful care,
    Affecting to seem unaffected.

With skill her eyes dart ev'ry glance,
    Yet change so soon you'd ne'er suspect them,
For she'd persuade they wound by chance,
    Tho' certain aim and art direct them.

430. linkin'] tripping.

She likes herself, yet others hates
    For that which in herself she prizes;
And, while she laughs at them, forgets
    She is the thing that she despises.

JOSEPH ADDISON

1672–1719

433.   *Hymn*

THE spacious firmament on high,
    With all the blue ethereal sky,
And spangled heavens, a shining frame,
Their great Original proclaim.
Th' unwearied Sun from day to day
Does his Creator's power display;
And publishes to every land
The work of an Almighty hand.

Soon as the evening shades prevail,
The Moon takes up the wondrous tale;
And nightly to the listening Earth
Repeats the story of her birth:
Whilst all the stars that round her burn,
And all the planets in their turn,
Confirm the tidings as they roll,
And spread the truth from pole to pole.

What though in solemn silence all
Move round the dark terrestrial ball;
What though nor real voice nor sound
Amidst their radiant orbs be found?
In Reason's ear they all rejoice,
And utter forth a glorious voice;
For ever singing as they shine,
'The Hand that made us is divine.'

ISAAC WATTS

1674–1748

434.   *The Day of Judgement*

WHEN the fierce North-wind with his airy forces
Rears up the Baltic to a foaming fury;
And the red lightning with a storm of hail comes
        Rushing amain down;

How the poor sailors stand amazed and tremble,
While the hoarse thunder, like a bloody trumpet,
Roars a loud onset to the gaping waters
        Quick to devour them.

Such shall the noise be, and the wild disorder
(If things eternal may be like these earthly),
Such the dire terror when the great Archangel
        Shakes the creation;

Tears the strong pillars of the vault of Heaven,
Breaks up old marble, the repose of princes,
Sees the graves open, and the bones arising,
        Flames all around them.

Hark, the shrill outcries of the guilty wretches!
Lively bright horror and amazing anguish
Stare thro' their eyelids, while the living worm lies
        Gnawing within them.

Thoughts, like old vultures, prey upon their heart-strings,
And the smart twinges, when the eye beholds the
Lofty Judge frowning, and a flood of vengeance
        Rolling afore him.

Hopeless immortals! how they scream and shiver,
While devils push them to the pit wide-yawning
Hideous and gloomy, to receive them headlong
        Down to the centre!

Stop here, my fancy: (all away, ye horrid
Doleful ideas!) come, arise to Jesus,
How He sits God-like! and the saints around Him
     Throned, yet adoring!

O may I sit there when He comes triumphant,
Dooming the nations! then ascend to glory,
While our Hosannas all along the passage
     Shout the Redeemer.

435.   ***A Cradle Hymn***

HUSH! my dear, lie still and slumber,
  Holy angels guard thy bed!
Heavenly blessings without number
  Gently falling on thy head.

Sleep, my babe; thy food and raiment,
  House and home, thy friends provide;
All without thy care or payment:
  All thy wants are well supplied.

How much better thou'rt attended
  Than the Son of God could be,
When from heaven He descended
  And became a child like thee!

Soft and easy is thy cradle:
  Coarse and hard thy Saviour lay,
When His birthplace was a stable
  And His softest bed was hay.

Blesséd babe! what glorious features—
  Spotless fair, divinely bright!
Must He dwell with brutal creatures?
  How could angels bear the sight?

Was there nothing but a manger
  Curséd sinners could afford

To receive the heavenly stranger?
　　Did they thus affront their Lord?

Soft, my child: I did not chide thee,
　　Though my song might sound too hard;
'Tis thy mother sits beside thee,
　　And her arms shall be thy guard.

Yet to read the shameful story
　　How the Jews abused their King,
How they served the Lord of Glory,
　　Makes me angry while I sing.

See the kinder shepherds round Him,
　　Telling wonders from the sky!
Where they sought Him, there they found Him,
　　With His Virgin mother by.

See the lovely babe a-dressing;
　　Lovely infant, how He smiled!
When He wept, the mother's blessing
　　Soothed and hush'd the holy child.

Lo, He slumbers in His manger,
　　Where the hornéd oxen fed:
Peace, my darling; here's no danger,
　　Here's no ox anear thy bed.

'Twas to save thee, child, from dying,
　　Save my dear from burning flame,
Bitter groans and endless crying,
　　That thy blest Redeemer came.

May'st thou live to know and fear Him,
　　Trust and love Him all thy days;
Then go dwell for ever near Him,
　　See His face, and sing His praise!

THOMAS PARNELL

1679–1718

436.   *Song*

WHEN thy beauty appears
        In its graces and airs
All bright as an angel new dropp'd from the sky,
At distance I gaze and am awed by my fears:
        So strangely you dazzle my eye!

        But when without art
        Your kind thoughts you impart,
When your love runs in blushes through every vein;
When it darts from your eyes, when it pants in your heart,
        Then I know you're a woman again.

        There's a passion and pride
        In our sex (she replied),
And thus, might I gratify both, I would do:
Still an angel appear to each lover beside,
        But still be a woman to you.

ALLAN RAMSAY

1686–1758

437.   *Peggy*

MY Peggy is a young thing,
        Just enter'd in her teens
Fair as the day, and sweet as May,
Fair as the day, and always gay;
        My Peggy is a young thing,
            And I'm not very auld,
        Yet well I like to meet her at
            The wawking of the fauld.

437. wawking] watching.

179

My Peggy speaks sae sweetly
    Whene'er we meet alane,
I wish nae mair to lay my care,
I wish nae mair of a' that's rare;
    My Peggy speaks sae sweetly,
        To a' the lave I'm cauld,
But she gars a' my spirits glow
        At wawking of the fauld.

My Peggy smiles sae kindly
    Whene'er I whisper love,
That I look down on a' the town,
That I look down upon a crown;
    My Peggy smiles sae kindly,
        It makes me blyth and bauld,
And naething gives me sic delight
        As wawking of the fauld.

My Peggy sings sae saftly
    When on my pipe I play,
By a' the rest it is confest,
By a' the rest, that she sings best;
    My Peggy sings sae saftly,
        And in her sangs are tauld
With innocence the wale of sense,
        At wawking of the fauld.

WILLIAM OLDYS

1687–1761

438. *On a Fly Drinking Out of His Cup*

BUSY, curious, thirsty fly!
    Drink with me and drink as I:
Freely welcome to my cup,

437. lave] rest. wale] choice.

Couldst thou sip and sip it up:
Make the most of life you may,
Life is short and wears away.

Both alike are mine and thine
Hastening quick to their decline:
Thine 's a summer, mine 's no more,
Though repeated to threescore.
Threescore summers, when they're gone,
Will appear as short as one!

JOHN GAY

1688–1732

439. *Song*

O RUDDIER than the cherry!
  O sweeter than the berry!
   O nymph more bright
   Than moonshine night,
Like kidlings blithe and merry!
Ripe as the melting cluster!
No lily has such lustre;
   Yet hard to tame
   As raging flame,
And fierce as storms that bluster!

ALEXANDER POPE

1688–1744

440. *On a Certain Lady at Court*

I KNOW a thing that 's most uncommon;
  (Envy, be silent and attend!)
I know a reasonable woman,
   Handsome and witty, yet a friend.

Not warp'd by passion, awed by rumour;
    Not grave through pride, nor gay through folly;
An equal mixture of good-humour
    And sensible soft melancholy.

'Has she no faults then (Envy says), Sir?'
    Yes, she has one, I must aver:
When all the world conspires to praise her,
    The woman's deaf, and does not hear.

441.   *Elegy to the Memory of an Unfortunate Lady*

WHAT beck'ning ghost, along the moonlight shade
    Invites my steps, and points to yonder glade?
'Tis she!—but why that bleeding bosom gored,
Why dimly gleams the visionary sword?
O, ever beauteous, ever friendly! tell,
Is it, in Heav'n, a crime to love too well?
To bear too tender or too firm a heart,
To act a lover's or a Roman's part?
Is there no bright reversion in the sky
For those who greatly think, or bravely die?
    Why bade ye else, ye Pow'rs! her soul aspire
Above the vulgar flight of low desire?
Ambition first sprung from your blest abodes;
The glorious fault of angels and of gods;
Thence to their images on earth it flows,
And in the breasts of kings and heroes glows.
Most souls, 'tis true, but peep out once an age,
Dull sullen pris'ners in the body's cage:
Dim lights of life, that burn a length of years,
Useless, unseen, as lamps in sepulchres;
Like Eastern kings a lazy state they keep,
And close confined to their own palace, sleep.

From these perhaps (ere Nature bade her die)
Fate snatch'd her early to the pitying sky.
As into air the purer spirits flow,
And sep'rate from their kindred dregs below,
So flew the soul to its congenial place,
Nor left one virtue to redeem her race.
But thou, false guardian of a charge too good!
Thou, mean deserter of thy brother's blood!
See on these ruby lips the trembling breath,
These cheeks now fading at the blast of Death:
Cold is that breast which warm'd the world before,
And those love-darting eyes must roll no more.
Thus, if eternal Justice rules the ball,
Thus shall your wives, and thus your children fall;
On all the line a sudden vengeance waits,
And frequent herses shall besiege your gates.
There passengers shall stand, and pointing say
(While the long fun'rals blacken all the way),
'Lo! these were they whose souls the Furies steel'd
And cursed with hearts unknowing how to yield.'
Thus unlamented pass the proud away,
The gaze of fools, and pageant of a day!
So perish all whose breast ne'er learn'd to glow
For others' good, or melt at others' woe!
What can atone (O ever-injured shade!)
Thy fate unpitied, and thy rites unpaid?
No friend's complaint, no kind domestic tear
Pleased thy pale ghost, or graced thy mournful bier.
By foreign hands thy dying eyes were closed,
By foreign hands thy decent limbs composed,
By foreign hands thy humble grave adorn'd,
By strangers honour'd, and by strangers mourn'd!
What tho' no friends in sable weeds appear,
Grieve for an hour, perhaps, then mourn a year,
And bear about the mockery of woe
To midnight dances, and the public show?

What tho' no weeping Loves thy ashes grace,
Nor polish'd marble emulate thy face?
What tho' no sacred earth allow thee room,
Nor hallow'd dirge be mutter'd o'er thy tomb?
Yet shall thy grave with rising flow'rs be drest,
And the green turf lie lightly on thy breast:
There shall the morn her earliest tears bestow,
There the first roses of the year shall blow;
While angels with their silver wings o'ershade
The ground now sacred by thy reliques made.

So peaceful rests, without a stone, a name,
What once had beauty, titles, wealth, and fame.
How loved, how honour'd once, avails thee not,
To whom related, or by whom begot;
A heap of dust alone remains of thee,
'Tis all thou art, and all the proud shall be!

Poets themselves must fall, like those they sung,
Deaf the praised ear, and mute the tuneful tongue.
Ev'n he, whose soul now melts in mournful lays,
Shall shortly want the gen'rous tear he pays;
Then from his closing eyes thy form shall part,
And the last pang shall tear thee from his heart;
Life's idle business at one gasp be o'er,
The Muse forgot, and thou beloved no more!

442.   *The Dying Christian to His Soul*

VITAL spark of heav'nly flame!
  Quit, O quit this mortal frame:
Trembling, hoping, ling'ring, flying,
  O the pain, the bliss of dying!
Cease, fond Nature, cease thy strife,
And let me languish into life.

Hark! they whisper; angels say,
Sister Spirit, come away!
What is this absorbs me quite?
Steals my senses, shuts my sight,
Drowns my spirits, draws my breath?
Tell me, my soul, can this be death?

The world recedes; it disappears!
Heav'n opens on my eyes! my ears
With sounds seraphic ring!
Lend, lend your wings! I mount! I fly!
O Grave! where is thy victory?
O Death! where is thy sting?

GEORGE BUBB DODINGTON, LORD MELCOMBE

1691?–1762

443.   *Shorten Sail*

LOVE thy country, wish it well,
    Not with too intense a care;
'Tis enough that, when it fell,
    Thou its ruin didst not share.

Envy's censure, Flattery's praise,
    With unmoved indifference view:
Learn to tread Life's dangerous maze
    With unerring Virtue's clue.

Void of strong desire and fear,
    Life's wide ocean trust no more;
Strive thy little bark to steer
    With the tide, but near the shore.

Thus prepared, thy shorten'd sail
    Shall, whene'er the winds increase,

Seizing each propitious gale,
    Waft thee to the port of Peace.

Keep thy conscience from offence
    And tempestuous passions free,
So, when thou art call'd from hence,
    Easy shall thy passage be.

—Easy shall thy passage be,
    Cheerful thy allotted stay,
Short the account 'twixt God and thee,
    Hope shall meet thee on thy way.

HENRY CAREY

1693?–1743

444.   *Sally in Our Alley*

OF all the girls that are so smart
    There's none like pretty Sally;
She is the darling of my heart,
    And she lives in our alley.
There is no lady in the land
    Is half so sweet as Sally;
She is the darling of my heart,
    And she lives in our alley.

Her father he makes cabbage-nets,
    And through the streets does cry 'em;
Her mother she sells laces long
    To such as please to buy 'em;
But sure such folks could ne'er beget
    So sweet a girl as Sally!
She is the darling of my heart,
    And she lives in our alley.

When she is by, I leave my work,
    I love her so sincerely;

My master comes like any Turk,
 And bangs me most severely:
But let him bang his bellyful,
 I'll bear it all for Sally;
She is the darling of my heart,
 And she lives in our alley.

Of all the days that's in the week
 I dearly love but one day—
And that's the day that comes betwixt
 A Saturday and Monday;
For then I'm drest all in my best
 To walk abroad with Sally;
She is the darling of my heart,
 And she lives in our alley.

My master carries me to church,
 And often am I blaméd
Because I leave him in the lurch
 As soon as text is naméd;
I leave the church in sermon-time
 And slink away to Sally;
She is the darling of my heart,
 And she lives in our alley.

When Christmas comes about again,
 O, then I shall have money;
I'll hoard it up, and box it all,
 I'll give it to my honey:
I would it were ten thousand pound,
 I'd give it all to Sally;
She is the darling of my heart,
 And she lives in our alley.

My master and the neighbors all
 Make game of me and Sally,

And, but for her, I'd better be
　　A slave and row a galley;
But when my seven long years are out,
　　O, then I'll marry Sally;
O, then we'll wed, and then we'll bed—
　　But not in our alley!

445.　　　*A Drinking-Song*

BACCHUS must now his power resign—
　　I am the only God of Wine!
It is not fit the wretch should be
In competition set with me,
Who can drink ten times more than he.

Make a new world, ye powers divine!
Stock'd with nothing else but Wine:
Let Wine its only product be,
Let Wine be earth, and air, and sea—
And let that Wine be all for me!

WILLIAM BROOME

?–1745

446.　　　*The Rosebud*

QUEEN of fragrance, lovely Rose,
　　The beauties of thy leaves disclose!
—But thou, fair Nymph, thyself survey
In this sweet offspring of a day.
That miracle of face must fail,
Thy charms are sweet, but charms are frail:
Swift as the short-lived flower they fly,
At morn they bloom, at evening die:

Though Sickness yet a while forbears,
Yet Time destroys what Sickness spares:
Now Helen lives alone in fame,
And Cleopatra's but a name:
Time must indent that heavenly brow,
And thou must be what they are now.

447. *Belinda's Recovery from Sickness*

THUS when the silent grave becomes
  Pregnant with life as fruitful wombs;
When the wide seas and spacious earth
    Resign us to our second birth;
Our moulder'd frame rebuilt assumes
New beauty, and for ever blooms,
And, crown'd with youth's immortal pride,
    We angels rise, who mortals died.

JAMES THOMSON

1700–1748

448. *On the Death of a Particular Friend*

AS those we love decay, we die in part,
  String after string is sever'd from the heart;
Till loosen'd life, at last but breathing clay,
Without one pang is glad to fall away.

Unhappy he who latest feels the blow!
Whose eyes have wept o'er every friend laid low,
Dragg'd ling'ring on from partial death to death,
Till, dying, all he can resign is—breath.

GEORGE LYTTELTON, LORD LYTTELTON

1709–1773

449. *Tell Me, My Heart, If This Be Love*

WHEN Delia on the plain appears,
Awed by a thousand tender fears
I would approach, but dare not move:
Tell me, my heart, if this be love?

Whene'er she speaks, my ravish'd ear
No other voice than hers can hear,
No other wit but hers approve:
Tell me, my heart, if this be love?

If she some other youth commend,
Though I was once his fondest friend,
His instant enemy I prove:
Tell me, my heart, if this be love?

When she is absent, I no more
Delight in all that pleased before—
The clearest spring, or shadiest grove:
Tell me, my heart, if this be love?

When fond of power, of beauty vain,
Her nets she spread for every swain,
I strove to hate, but vainly strove:
Tell me, my heart, if this be love?

SAMUEL JOHNSON

1709–1784

450.   *One-and-Twenty*

LONG-EXPECTED one-and-twenty,
    Ling'ring year, at length is flown:
Pride and pleasure, pomp and plenty,
    Great * * *   * * * *, are now your own.

Loosen'd from the minor's tether,
    Free to mortgage or to sell,
Wild as wind and light as feather,
    Bid the sons of thrift farewell.

Call the Betsies, Kates, and Jennies,
    All the names that banish care;
Lavish of your grandsire's guineas,
    Show the spirit of an heir.

All that prey on vice and folly
    Joy to see their quarry fly:
There the gamester, light and jolly,
    There the lender, grave and sly.

Wealth, my lad, was made to wander,
    Let it wander as it will;
Call the jockey, call the pander,
    Bid them come and take their fill.

When the bonny blade carouses,
    Pockets full, and spirits high—
What are acres? What are houses?
    Only dirt, or wet or dry.

Should the guardian friend or mother
    Tell the woes of wilful waste,
Scorn their counsel, scorn their pother;—
    You can hang or drown at last!

451. On the Death of Mr. Robert Levet, a Practiser in Physic

CONDEMN'D to Hope's delusive mine,
  As on we toil from day to day,
By sudden blasts or slow decline
  Our social comforts drop away.

Well tried through many a varying year,
  See Levet to the grave descend,
Officious, innocent, sincere,
  Of every friendless name the friend.

Yet still he fills affection's eye,
  Obscurely wise and coarsely kind;
Nor, letter'd Arrogance, deny
  Thy praise to merit unrefined.

When fainting nature call'd for aid,
  And hov'ring death prepared the blow,
His vig'rous remedy display'd
  The power of art without the show.

In Misery's darkest cavern known,
  His useful care was ever nigh,
Where hopeless Anguish pour'd his groan,
  And lonely Want retired to die.

No summons mock'd by chill delay,
  No petty gain disdain'd by pride;
The modest wants of every day
  The toil of every day supplied.

His virtues walk'd their narrow round,
  Nor made a pause, nor left a void;
And sure th' Eternal Master found
  The single talent well employ'd.

The busy day, the peaceful night,
   Unfelt, uncounted, glided by;
His frame was firm—his powers were bright,
   Though now his eightieth year was nigh.

Then with no fiery throbbing pain,
   No cold gradations of decay,
Death broke at once the vital chain,
   And freed his soul the nearest way.

RICHARD JAGO

1715–1781

452. *Absence*

WITH leaden foot Time creeps along
   While Delia is away:
With her, nor plaintive was the song,
   Nor tedious was the day.

Ah, envious Pow'r! reverse my doom;
   Now double thy career,
Strain ev'ry nerve, stretch ev'ry plume,
   And rest them when she's here!

THOMAS GRAY

1716–1771

453. *Elegy Written in a Country Churchyard*

THE Curfew tolls the knell of parting day,
   The lowing herd wind slowly o'er the lea,
The plowman homeward plods his weary way,
   And leaves the world to darkness and to me.

Now fades the glimmering landscape on the sight,
    And all the air a solemn stillness holds,
Save where the beetle wheels his droning flight,
    And drowsy tinklings lull the distant folds:

Save that from yonder ivy-mantled tow'r
    The moping owl does to the moon complain
Of such as, wand'ring near her secret bow'r,
    Molest her ancient solitary reign.

Beneath those rugged elms, that yew-tree's shade,
    Where heaves the turf in many a mould'ring heap,
Each in his narrow cell for ever laid,
    The rude Forefathers of the hamlet sleep.

The breezy call of incense-breathing Morn,
    The swallow twitt'ring from the straw-built shed,
The cock's shrill clarion, or the echoing horn,
    No more shall rouse them from their lowly bed.

For them no more the blazing hearth shall burn,
    Or busy housewife ply her evening care:
No children run to lisp their sire's return,
    Or climb his knees the envied kiss to share.

Oft did the harvest to their sickle yield,
    Their furrow oft the stubborn glebe has broke:
How jocund did they drive their team afield!
    How bow'd the woods beneath their sturdy stroke!

Let not Ambition mock their useful toil,
    Their homely joys, and destiny obscure;
Nor Grandeur hear with a disdainful smile
    The short and simple annals of the poor.

The boast of heraldry, the pomp of pow'r,
    And all that beauty, all that wealth e'er gave,
Await alike th' inevitable hour:
    The paths of glory lead but to the grave.

Nor you, ye proud, impute to these the fault,
    If Memory o'er their tomb no Trophies raise,
Where through the long-drawn aisle and fretted vault
    The pealing anthem swells the note of praise.

Can storied urn or animated bust
    Back to its mansion call the fleeting breath?
Can Honour's voice provoke the silent dust,
    Or Flatt'ry soothe the dull cold ear of death?

Perhaps in this neglected spot is laid
    Some heart once pregnant with celestial fire;
Hands, that the rod of empire might have sway'd,
    Or waked to ecstasy the living lyre.

But Knowledge to their eyes her ample page
    Rich with the spoils of time did ne'er unroll;
Chill Penury repress'd their noble rage,
    And froze the genial current of the soul.

Full many a gem of purest ray serene
    The dark unfathom'd caves of ocean bear:
Full many a flower is born to blush unseen,
    And waste its sweetness on the desert air.

Some village Hampden that with dauntless breast
    The little tyrant of his fields withstood,
Some mute inglorious Milton here may rest,
    Some Cromwell guiltless of his country's blood.

Th' applause of list'ning senates to command,
    The threats of pain and ruin to despise,
To scatter plenty o'er a smiling land,
    And read their history in a nation's eyes—

Their lot forbade: nor circumscribed alone
    Their growing virtues, but their crimes confined;
Forbade to wade thro' slaughter to a throne,
    And shut the gates of mercy on mankind,

The struggling pangs of conscious truth to hide,
    To quench the blushes of ingenuous shame,
Or heap the shrine of Luxury and Pride
    With incense kindled at the Muse's flame.

Far from the madding crowd's ignoble strife,
    Their sober wishes never learn'd to stray;
Along the cool sequester'd vale of life
    They kept the noiseless tenor of their way.

Yet ev'n these bones from insult to protect
    Some frail memorial still erected nigh,
With uncouth rhymes and shapeless sculpture deck'd,
    Implores the passing tribute of a sigh.

Their name, their years, spelt by th' unletter'd muse,
    The place of fame and elegy supply:
And many a holy text around she strews,
    That teach the rustic moralist to die.

For who, to dumb Forgetfulness a prey,
    This pleasing anxious being e'er resign'd,
Left the warm precincts of the cheerful day,
    Nor cast one longing ling'ring look behind?

On some fond breast the parting soul relies,
    Some pious drops the closing eye requires;
Ee'n from the tomb the voice of Nature cries,
    Ee'n in our Ashes live their wonted Fires.

For thee, who, mindful of th' unhonour'd dead,
    Dost in these lines their artless tale relate;
If chance, by lonely contemplation led,
    Some kindred spirit shall inquire thy fate—

Haply some hoary-headed Swain may say,
    'Oft have we seen him at the peep of dawn
Brushing with hasty steps the dews away
    To meet the sun upon the upland lawn.

'There at the foot of yonder nodding beech
　　That wreathes its old fantastic roots so high,
His listless length at noontide would he stretch,
　　And pore upon the brook that babbles by.

'Hard by yon wood, now smiling as in scorn,
　　Mutt'ring his wayward fancies he would rove,
Now drooping, woeful wan, like one forlorn,
　　Or crazed with care, or cross'd in hopeless love.

'One morn I miss'd him on the custom'd hill,
　　Along the heath and near his fav'rite tree;
Another came; nor yet beside the rill,
　　Nor up the lawn, nor at the wood was he;

'The next with dirges due in sad array
　　Slow through the church-way path we saw him borne.
Approach and read (for thou canst read) the lay
　　Graved on the stone beneath yon aged thorn:'

THE EPITAPH

Here rests his head upon the lap of Earth
　　A Youth to Fortune and to Fame unknown.
Fair Science frown'd not on his humble birth,
　　And Melancholy mark'd him for her own.

Large was his bounty, and his soul sincere,
　　Heav'n did a recompense as largely send:
He gave to Mis'ry all he had, a tear,
　　He gain'd from Heav'n ('twas all he wish'd) a friend.

No farther seek his merits to disclose,
　　Or draw his frailties from their dread abode,
(There they alike in trembling hope repose,)
　　The bosom of his Father and his God.

454.   *The Curse upon Edward*

WEAVE the warp, and weave the woof,
    The winding-sheet of Edward's race.
Give ample room, and verge enough
The characters of hell to trace.
Mark the year, and mark the night,
When Severn shall re-echo with affright
The shrieks of death, thro' Berkley's roofs that ring,
Shrieks of an agonizing King!
    She-wolf of France, with unrelenting fangs,
That tear'st the bowels of thy mangled mate,
    From thee be born, who o'er thy country hangs
The scourge of Heav'n. What terrors round him wait!
Amazement in his van, with Flight combined,
And Sorrow's faded form, and Solitude behind.

    Mighty Victor, mighty Lord!
Low on his funeral couch he lies!
    No pitying heart, no eye, afford
A tear to grace his obsequies.
Is the sable warrior fled?
Thy son is gone. He rests among the dead.
The swarm that in thy noon tide beam were born?
Gone to salute the rising morn.
Fair laughs the morn, and soft the zephyr blows,
While proudly riding o'er the azure realm
In gallant trim the gilded vessel goes;
    Youth on the prow, and Pleasure at the helm;
Regardless of the sweeping whirlwind's sway,
That, hush'd in grim repose, expects his evening prey.

    Fill high the sparkling bowl,
The rich repast prepare;
    Reft of a crown, he yet may share the feast:
Close by the regal chair

Fell Thirst and Famine scowl
A baleful smile upon their baffled guest.
Heard ye the din of battle bray,
    Lance to lance, and horse to horse?
    Long years of havoc urge their destined course,
And thro' the kindred squadrons mow their way.
    Ye Towers of Julius, London's lasting shame,
With many a foul and midnight murder fed,
    Revere his consort's faith, his father's fame,
And spare the meek usurper's holy head.
Above, below, the rose of snow,
    Twined with her blushing foe, we spread:
The bristled boar in infant-gore
    Wallows beneath the thorny shade.
Now, brothers, bending o'er th' accursèd loom
Stamp we our vengeance deep, and ratify his doom.

    Edward, lo! to sudden fate
(Weave we the woof. The thread is spun)
    Half of thy heart we consecrate.
(The web is wove. The work is done.)

455.   *The Progress of Poesy*

A Pindaric Ode

AWAKE, Æolian lyre, awake,
    And give to rapture all thy trembling strings,
From Helicon's harmonious springs
    A thousand rills their mazy progress take:
The laughing flowers, that round them blow,
Drink life and fragrance as they flow.
Now the rich stream of music winds along
Deep, majestic, smooth and strong,
Thro' verdant vales, and Ceres' golden reign:
Now rolling down the steep amain,

Headlong, impetuous, see it pour;
The rocks and nodding groves rebellow to the roar.

    O Sovereign of the willing soul,
Parent of sweet and solemn-breathing airs,
Enchanting shell! the sullen Cares
    And frantic Passions hear thy soft controul.
On Thracia's hills the Lord of War
Has curb'd the fury of his car,
And dropp'd his thirsty lance at thy command.
Perching on the sceptred hand
Of Jove, thy magic lulls the feather'd king
With ruffled plumes and flagging wing:
Quench'd in dark clouds of slumber lie
The terror of his beak, and lightnings of his eye.

Thee the voice, the dance, obey,
Temper'd to thy warbled lay.
    O'er Idalia's velvet-green
    The rosy-crownéd Loves are seen
On Cytherea's day
    With antic Sports, and blue-eyed Pleasures,
    Frisking light in frolic measures;
Now pursuing, now retreating,
    Now in circling troops they meet:
To brisk notes in cadence beating,
    Glance their many-twinkling feet.
Slow melting strains their Queen's approach declare:
    Where'er she turns the Graces homage pay.
With arms sublime, that float upon the air,
    In gliding state she wins her easy way:
O'er her warm cheek and rising bosom move
The bloom of young Desire and purple light of Love.

    Man's feeble race what ills await,
Labour, and Penury, the racks of Pain,
    Disease, and Sorrow's weeping train,

And Death, sad refuge from the storms of fate!
The fond complaint, my song, disprove,
And justify the laws of Jove.
Say, has he giv'n in vain the heav'nly Muse?
Night, and all her sickly dews,
Her sceptres wan, and birds of boding cry,
He gives to range the dreary sky:
Till down the eastern cliffs afar
Hyperion's march they spy, and glitt'ring shafts of war.

    In climes beyond the solar road,
Where shaggy forms o'er ice-built mountains roam,
The Muse has broke the twilight gloom
    To cheer the shiv'ring native's dull abode,
And oft, beneath the od'rous shade
Of Chili's boundless forests laid,
She deigns to hear the savage youth repeat
In loose numbers wildly sweet
Their feather-cinctured chiefs, and dusky loves.
Her track, where'er the Goddess roves,
Glory pursue and generous Shame,
Th' unconquerable Mind, and Freedom's holy flame.

Woods, that wave o'er Delphi's steep,
Isles, that crown th' Ægean deep,
    Fields, that cool Ilissus laves,
    Or where Mæander's amber waves
In lingering lab'rinths creep,
    How do your tuneful echoes languish,
    Mute, but to the voice of anguish?
Where each old poetic mountain
    Inspiration breathed around:
Ev'ry shade and hallow'd fountain
    Murmur'd deep a solemn sound:
Till the sad Nine, in Greece's evil hour,
    Left their Parnassus for the Latian plains.
Alike they scorn the pomp of tyrant Power,

And coward Vice, that revels in her chains.
When Latium had her lofty spirit lost,
They sought, O Albion! next, thy sea-encircled coast.

    Far from the sun and summer gale,
In thy green lap was Nature's darling laid,
What time, where lucid Avon stray'd,
    To Him the mighty mother did unveil
Her awful face: the dauntless child
Stretch'd forth his little arms, and smiled.
This pencil take (she said), whose colours clear
Richly paint the vernal year:
Thine too these golden keys, immortal boy!
This can unlock the gates of joy;
Of horror that, and thrilling fears,
Or ope the sacred source of sympathetic tears.

    Nor second he, that rode sublime
Upon the seraph-wings of Ecstasy,
The secrets of th' abyss to spy.
    He pass'd the flaming bounds of place and time:
The living Throne, the sapphire-blaze,
Where Angels tremble while they gaze,
He saw; but blasted with excess of light,
Closed his eyes in endless night.
Behold, where Dryden's less presumptuous car,
Wide o'er the fields of glory bear
Two coursers of ethereal race,
With necks in thunder clothed, and long-resounding pace.

Hark, his hands the lyre explore!
Bright-eyed Fancy hovering o'er
    Scatters from her pictured urn
    Thoughts that breathe, and words that burn.
But ah! 'tis heard no more——
    O Lyre divine! what daring Spirit
    Wakes thee now? Tho' he inherit

Nor the pride, nor ample pinion,
  That the Theban eagle bear
Sailing with supreme dominion
  Thro' the azure deep of air:
Yet oft before his infant eyes would run
  Such forms as glitter in the Muse's ray,
With orient hues, unborrow'd of the Sun:
  Yet shall he mount, and keep his distant way
Beyond the limits of a vulgar fate,
Beneath the Good how far—but far above the Great.

**456. *On a Favourite Cat, Drowned
        in a Tub of Gold Fishes***

'TWAS on a lofty vase's side,
    Where China's gayest art had dyed
  The azure flowers that blow;
Demurest of the tabby kind,
The pensive Selima reclined,
    Gazed on the lake below.

Her conscious tail her joy declared;
The fair round face, the snowy beard,
    The velvet of her paws,
Her coat, that with the tortoise vies,
Her ears of jet, and emerald eyes,
    She saw; and purr'd applause.

Still had she gazed; but 'midst the tide
Two angel forms were seen to glide,
    The Genii of the stream:
Their scaly armour's Tyrian hue
Thro' richest purple to the view
    Betray'd a golden gleam.

The hapless Nymph with wonder saw:
A whisker first and then a claw,

With many an ardent wish,
She stretch'd in vain to reach the prize.
What female heart can gold despise?
　　What Cat 's averse to fish?

Presumptuous Maid! with looks intent
Again she stretch'd, again she bent,
　　Nor knew the gulf between.
(Malignant Fate sat by, and smiled.)
The slipp'ry verge her feet beguiled,
　　She tumbled headlong in.

Eight times emerging from the flood
She mew'd to ev'ry wat'ry god,
　　Some speedy aid to send.
No Dolphin came, no Nereid stirr'd:
Nor cruel *Tom*, nor *Susan* heard.
　　A Fav'rite has no friend!

From hence, ye Beauties, undeceived,
Know, one false step is ne'er retrieved,
　　And be with caution bold.
Not all that tempts your wand'ring eyes
And heedless hearts, is lawful prize;
　　Nor all that glisters, gold.

WILLIAM COLLINS

1721–1759

457.　　*Ode to Simplicity*

O THOU, by Nature taught
　　To breathe her genuine thought
In numbers warmly pure and sweetly strong:
　　Who first on mountains wild,
　　In Fancy, loveliest child,
Thy babe and Pleasure's, nursed the pow'rs of song!

Thou, who with hermit heart
Disdain'st the wealth of art,
And gauds, and pageant weeds, and trailing pall:
But com'st a decent maid,
In Attic robe array'd,
O chaste, unboastful nymph, to thee I call!

By all the honey'd store
On Hybla's thymy shore,
By all her blooms and mingled murmurs dear,
By her whose love-lorn woe,
In evening musings slow,
Soothed sweetly sad Electra's poet's ear:

By old Cephisus deep,
Who spread his wavy sweep
In warbled wand'rings round thy green retreat;
On whose enamell'd side,
When holy Freedom died,
No equal haunt allured thy future feet!

O sister meek of Truth,
To my admiring youth
Thy sober aid and native charms infuse!
The flow'rs that sweetest breathe,
Though beauty cull'd the wreath,
Still ask thy hand to range their order'd hues.

While Rome could none esteem,
But virtue's patriot theme,
You loved her hills, and led her laureate band;
But stay'd to sing alone
To one distinguish'd throne,
And turn'd thy face, and fled her alter'd land.

No more, in hall or bow'r,
The passions own thy pow'r.
Love, only Love her forceless numbers mean;

For thou hast left her shrine,
Nor olive more, nor vine,
Shall gain thy feet to bless the servile scene.

Though taste, though genius bless
To some divine excess,
Faint 's the cold work till thou inspire the whole;
What each, what all supply,
May court, may charm our eye,
Thou, only thou, canst raise the meeting soul!

Of these let others ask,
To aid some mighty task,
I only seek to find thy temperate vale;
Where oft my reed might sound
To maids and shepherds round,
And all thy sons, O Nature, learn my tale.

458.   *How Sleep the Brave*

HOW sleep the brave, who sink to rest
By all their country's wishes blest!
When Spring, with dewy fingers cold,
Returns to deck their hallow'd mould,
She there shall dress a sweeter sod
Than Fancy's feet have ever trod.

By fairy hands their knell is rung;
By forms unseen their dirge is sung;
There Honour comes, a pilgrim grey,
To bless the turf that wraps their clay;
And Freedom shall awhile repair
To dwell, a weeping hermit, there!

459.   *Ode to Evening*

IF aught of oaten stop, or pastoral song,
  May hope, chaste Eve, to soothe thy modest ear,
    Like thy own solemn springs,
    Thy springs and dying gales;

O nymph reserved, while now the bright-hair'd sun
Sits in yon western tent, whose cloudy skirts,
    With brede ethereal wove,
    O'erhang his wavy bed:

Now air is hush'd, save where the weak-eyed bat
With short shrill shriek flits by on leathern wing,
    Or where the beetle winds
    His small but sullen horn,

As oft he rises, 'midst the twilight path
Against the pilgrim borne in heedless hum:
    Now teach me, maid composed,
    To breathe some soften'd strain,

Whose numbers, stealing through thy darkening vale,
May not unseemly with its stillness suit,
    As, musing slow, I hail
    Thy genial loved return!

For when thy folding-star arising shows
His paly circlet, at his warning lamp
    The fragrant hours, and elves
    Who slept in buds the day,

And many a nymph who wreathes her brows with sedge,
And sheds the freshening dew, and, lovelier still,
    The pensive pleasures sweet,
    Prepare thy shadowy car:

Then lead, calm votaress, where some sheety lake
Cheers the lone heath, or some time-hallow'd pile,
    Or upland fallows grey
    Reflect its last cool gleam.

Or if chill blustering winds, or driving rain,
Prevent my willing feet, be mine the hut
    That from the mountain's side
    Views wilds and swelling floods,

And hamlets brown, and dim-discover'd spires,
And hears their simple bell, and marks o'er all
    Thy dewy fingers draw
    The gradual dusky veil.

While Spring shall pour his show'rs, as oft he wont,
And bathe thy breathing tresses, meekest Eve!
    While Summer loves to sport
    Beneath thy lingering light;

While sallow Autumn fills thy lap with leaves,
Or Winter, yelling through the troublous air,
    Affrights thy shrinking train,
    And rudely rends thy robes:

So long, regardful of thy quiet rule,
Shall Fancy, Friendship, Science, rose-lipp'd Health
    Thy gentlest influence own,
    And hymn thy favourite name!

460. *Fidele*

TO fair Fidele's grassy tomb
    Soft maids and village hinds shall bring
Each opening sweet of earliest bloom,
    And rifle all the breathing Spring.

No wailing ghost shall dare appear
   To vex with shrieks this quiet grove;
But shepherd lads assemble here,
   And melting virgins own their love.

No wither'd witch shall here be seen,
   No goblins lead their nightly crew;
The female fays shall haunt the green,
   And dress thy grave with pearly dew.

The redbreast oft at evening hours
   Shall kindly lend his little aid,
With hoary moss, and gather'd flowers,
   To deck the ground where thou art laid.

When howling winds, and beating rain,
   In tempests shake thy sylvan cell;
Or 'midst the chase, on every plain,
   The tender thought on thee shall dwell;

Each lonely scene shall thee restore,
   For thee the tear be duly shed;
Beloved, till life can charm no more;
   And mourn'd till Pity's self be dead.

MARK AKENSIDE

1721–1770

461.   *Amoret*

IF rightly tuneful bards decide,
   If it be fix'd in Love's decrees,
That Beauty ought not to be tried
   But by its native power to please,
Then tell me, youths and lovers, tell—
What fair can Amoret excel?

Behold that bright unsullied smile,
　　And wisdom speaking in her mien:
Yet—she so artless all the while,
　　So little studious to be seen—
We naught but instant gladness know,
Nor think to whom the gift we owe.

But neither music, nor the powers
　　Of youth and mirth and frolic cheer,
Add half the sunshine to the hours,
　　Or make life's prospect half so clear,
As memory brings it to the eye
From scenes where Amoret was by.

This, sure, is Beauty's happiest part;
　　This gives the most unbounded sway;
This shall enchant the subject heart
　　When rose and lily fade away;
And she be still, in spite of Time,
Sweet Amoret in all her prime.

462. *The Complaint*

A WAY! away!
　　Tempt me no more, insidious Love:
　Thy soothing sway
Long did my youthful bosom prove:
At length thy treason is discern'd,
At length some dear-bought caution earn'd:
Away! nor hope my riper age to move.

　　I know, I see
Her merit. Needs it now be shown,
　　Alas! to me?
How often, to myself unknown,
The graceful, gentle, virtuous maid
Have I admired! How often said—
What joy to call a heart like hers one's own!

But, flattering god,
O squanderer of content and ease
    In thy abode
Will care's rude lesson learn to please?
O say, deceiver, hast thou won
Proud Fortune to attend thy throne,
Or placed thy friends above her stern decrees?

463.   *The Nightingale*

TO-NIGHT retired, the queen of heaven
    With young Endymion stays;
And now to Hesper it is given
Awhile to rule the vacant sky,
Till she shall to her lamp supply
    A stream of brighter rays.

Propitious send thy golden ray,
    Thou purest light above!
Let no false flame seduce to stray
Where gulf or steep lie hid for harm;
But lead where music's healing charm
    May soothe afflicted love.

To them, by many a grateful song
    In happier seasons vow'd,
These lawns, Olympia's haunts, belong:
Oft by yon silver stream we walk'd,
Or fix'd, while Philomela talk'd,
    Beneath yon copses stood.

Nor seldom, where the beechen boughs
    That roofless tower invade,
We came, while her enchanting Muse
The radiant moon above us held:
Till, by a clamorous owl compell'd,
    She fled the solemn shade.

But hark! I hear her liquid tone!
    Now Hesper guide my feet!
Down the red marl with moss o'ergrown,
Through yon wild thicket next the plain,
Whose hawthorns choke the winding lane
    Which leads to her retreat.

See the green space: on either hand
    Enlarged it spreads around:
See, in the midst she takes her stand,
Where one old oak his awful shade
Extends o'er half the level mead,
    Enclosed in woods profound.

Hark! how through many a melting note
    She now prolongs her lays:
How sweetly down the void they float!
The breeze their magic path attends;
The stars shine out; the forest bends;
    The wakeful heifers graze.

Whoe'er thou art whom chance may bring
    To this sequester'd spot,
If then the plaintive Siren sing,
O softly tread beneath her bower
And think of Heaven's disposing power,
    Of man's uncertain lot.

O think, o'er all this mortal stage
    What mournful scenes arise:
What ruin waits on kingly rage;
How often virtue dwells with woe;
How many griefs from knowledge flow;
    How swiftly pleasure flies!

O sacred bird! let me at eve,
Thus wandering all alone,
Thy tender counsel oft receive,
Bear witness to thy pensive airs,
And pity Nature's common cares,
Till I forget my own.

TOBIAS GEORGE SMOLLETT

1721–1771

464. *To Leven Water*

PURE stream, in whose transparent wave
My youthful limbs I wont to lave;
No torrents stain thy limpid source,
No rocks impede thy dimpling course.
Devolving from thy parent lake
A charming maze thy waters make
By bowers of birch and groves of pine
And edges flower'd with eglantine.

Still on thy banks so gaily green
May numerous herds and flocks be seen,
And lasses chanting o'er the pail,
And shepherds piping in the dale,
And ancient faith that knows no guile,
And industry embrown'd with toil,
And hearts resolved and hands prepared
The blessings they enjoy to guard.

CHRISTOPHER SMART

1722–1770

465.   *Song to David*

SUBLIME—invention ever young,
    Of vast conception, tow'ring tongue
        To God th' eternal theme;
Notes from yon exaltations caught,
Unrivall'd royalty of thought
        O'er meaner strains supreme.

His muse, bright angel of his verse,
Gives balm for all the thorns that pierce,
        For all the pangs that rage;
Blest light still gaining on the gloom,
The more than Michal of his bloom,
        Th' Abishag of his age.

He sang of God—the mighty source
Of all things—the stupendous force
        On which all strength depends;
From whose right arm, beneath whose eyes,
All period, power, and enterprise
        Commences, reigns, and ends.

Tell them, I AM, Jehovah said
To Moses; while earth heard in dread,
        And, smitten to the heart,
At once above, beneath, around,
All Nature, without voice or sound,
        Replied, O LORD, THOU ART.

The world, the clustering spheres, He made;
The glorious light, the soothing shade,
        Dale, champaign, grove, and hill;

The multitudinous abyss,
Where Secrecy remains in bliss,
 And Wisdom hides her skill.

The pillars of the Lord are seven,
Which stand from earth to topmost heaven;
 His Wisdom drew the plan;
His Word accomplish'd the design,
From brightest gem to deepest mine;
 From Christ enthroned, to Man.

For Adoration all the ranks
Of Angels yield eternal thanks,
 And David in the midst;
With God's good poor, which, last and least
In man's esteem, Thou to Thy feast,
 O blessèd Bridegroom, bidd'st!

For Adoration, David's Psalms
Lift up the heart to deeds of alms;
 And he, who kneels and chants,
Prevails his passions to control,
Finds meat and medicine to the soul,
 Which for translation pants.

For Adoration, in the dome
Of Christ, the sparrows find a home,
 And on His olives perch:
The swallow also dwells with thee,
O man of God's humility,
 Within his Saviour's church.

Sweet is the dew that falls betimes,
And drops upon the leafy limes;
 Sweet Hermon's fragrant air:
Sweet is the lily's silver bell,
And sweet the wakeful tapers' smell
 That watch for early prayer.

215

Sweet the young nurse, with love intense,
Which smiles o'er sleeping innocence;
    Sweet, when the lost arrive:
Sweet the musician's ardour beats,
While his vague mind 's in quest of sweets,
    The choicest flowers to hive.

Strong is the horse upon his speed;
Strong in pursuit the rapid glede,
    Which makes at once his game:
Strong the tall ostrich on the ground;
Strong through the turbulent profound
    Shoots Xiphias to his aim.

Strong is the lion—like a coal
His eyeball,—like a bastion's mole
    His chest against the foes:
Strong the gier-eagle on his sail;
Strong against tide th' enormous whale
    Emerges as he goes.

But stronger still, in earth and air,
And in the sea, the man of prayer,
    And far beneath the tide:
And in the seat to faith assign'd,
Where ask is have, where seek is find,
    Where knock is open wide.

Precious the penitential tear;
And precious is the sigh sincere,
    Acceptable to God:
And precious are the winning flowers,
In gladsome Israel's feast of bowers
    Bound on the hallow'd sod.

glede] kite.   Xiphias] sword-fish.

Glorious the sun in mid career;
Glorious th' assembled fires appear;
　　Glorious the comet's train:
Glorious the trumpet and alarm;
Glorious the Almighty's stretch'd-out arm;
　　Glorious th' enraptured main:

Glorious the northern lights astream;
Glorious the song, when God 's the theme;
　　Glorious the thunder's roar:
Glorious Hosanna from the den;
Glorious the catholic Amen;
　　Glorious the martyr's gore:

Glorious—more glorious—is the crown
Of Him that brought salvation down,
　　By meekness call'd thy Son:
Thou that stupendous truth believed;—
And now the matchless deed's achieved,
　　Determined, dared, and done!

JANE ELLIOT

1727–1805

466.　　*A Lament for Flodden*

I'VE heard them lilting at our ewe-milking,
　　Lasses a' lilting before dawn o' day;
But now they are moaning on ilka green loaning—
　　The Flowers of the Forest are a' wede away.

At bughts, in the morning, nae blythe lads are scorning,
　　Lasses are lonely and dowie and wae;
Nae daffing, nae gabbing, but sighing and sabbing,
　　Ilk ane lifts her leglin and hies her away.

466. loaning] lane, field-track.　wede] weeded.
bughts] sheep-folds.　daffing] joking.　leglin] milk-pail.

In hairst, at the shearing, nae youths now are jeering,
    Bandsters are lyart, and runkled, and gray:
At fair or at preaching, nae wooing, nae fleeching—
    The Flowers of the Forest are a' wede away.

At e'en, in the gloaming, nae swankies are roaming
    'Bout stacks wi' the lasses at bogle to play;
But ilk ane sits eerie, lamenting her dearie—
    The Flowers of the Forest are a' wede away.

Dool and wae for the order sent our lads to the Border!
    The English, for ance, by guile wan the day;
The Flowers of the Forest, that fought aye the foremost,
    The prime of our land, lie cauld in the clay.

We'll hear nae mair lilting at our ewe-milking;
    Women and bairns are heartless and wae;
Sighing and moaning on ilka green loaning—
    The Flowers of the Forest are a' wede away.

OLIVER GOLDSMITH

1728–1774

467.   *Woman*

WHEN lovely woman stoops to folly,
    And finds too late that men betray,
What charm can soothe her melancholy?
    What art can wash her tears away?

The only art her guilt to cover,
    To hide her shame from ev'ry eye,
To give repentance to her lover,
    And wring his bosom is—to die.

466. hairst] harvest.   bandsters] binders.
lyart] gray-haired.   runkled] wrinkled.
fleeching] coaxing.   swankies] lusty lads.
bogle] bogy, hide-and-seek.   dool] mourning.

468.   *Memory*

O MEMORY, thou fond deceiver,
    Still importunate and vain,
To former joys recurring ever,
    And turning all the past to pain:

Thou, like the world, th' oppress'd oppressing,
    Thy smiles increase the wretch's woe:
And he who wants each other blessing
    In thee must ever find a foe.

ROBERT CUNNINGHAME-GRAHAM OF GARTMORE

1735–1797

469.   *If Doughty Deeds*

IF doughty deeds my lady please,
    Right soon I'll mount my steed;
And strong his arm and fast his seat,
    That bears frae me the meed.
I'll wear thy colours in my cap,
    Thy picture in my heart;
And he that bends not to thine eye
    Shall rue it to his smart!
       Then tell me how to woo thee, Love;
        O tell me how to woo thee!
       For thy dear sake nae care I'll take,
        Tho' ne'er another trow me.

If gay attire delight thine eye
    I'll dight me in array;
I'll tend thy chamber door all night,
    And squire thee all the day.
If sweetest sounds can win thine ear,
    These sounds I'll strive to catch;

Thy voice I'll steal to woo thysel',
   That voice that nane can match.
      Then tell me how to woo thee, Love. . .

But if fond love thy heart can gain,
   I never broke a vow;
Nae maiden lays her skaith to me,
   I never loved but you.
For you alone I ride the ring,
   For you I wear the blue;
For you alone I strive to sing,
   O tell me how to woo!
      Then tell me how to woo thee, Love;
        O tell me how to woo thee!
      For thy dear sake nae care I'll take
      Tho' ne'er another trow me.

WILLIAM COWPER

1731–1800

470.   *To Mary Unwin*

MARY! I want a lyre with other strings,
   Such aid from Heaven as some have feign'd they drew,
An eloquence scarce given to mortals, new
And undebased by praise of meaner things;
That ere through age or woe I shed my wings,
I may record thy worth with honour due,
In verse as musical as thou art true,
And that immortalizes whom it sings:
But thou hast little need. There is a Book
By seraphs writ with beams of heavenly light,
On which the eyes of God not rarely look,
A chronicle of actions just and bright—
   There all thy deeds, my faithful Mary, shine;
   And since thou own'st that praise, I spare thee mine.

471.   *My Mary*

THE twentieth year is wellnigh past
  Since first our sky was overcast;
Ah, would that this might be the last!
                    My Mary!

Thy spirits have a fainter flow,
I see thee daily weaker grow;
'Twas my distress that brought thee low,
                    My Mary!

Thy needles, once a shining store,
For my sake restless heretofore,
Now rust disused, and shine no more;
                    My Mary!

For though thou gladly wouldst fulfil
The same kind office for me still,
Thy sight now seconds not thy will,
                    My Mary!

But well thou play'dst the housewife's part,
And all thy threads with magic art
Have wound themselves about this heart,
                    My Mary!

Thy indistinct expressions seem
Like language utter'd in a dream;
Yet me they charm, whate'er the theme,
                    My Mary!

Thy silver locks, once auburn bright,
Are still more lovely in my sight
Than golden beams of orient light,
                    My Mary!

For could I view nor them nor thee,
What sight worth seeing could I see?
The sun would rise in vain for me,
> My Mary!

Partakers of thy sad decline,
Thy hands their little force resign;
Yet, gently press'd, press gently mine,
> My Mary!

Such feebleness of limbs thou prov'st,
That now at every step thou mov'st
Upheld by two; yet still thou lov'st,
> My Mary!

And still to love, though press'd with ill,
In wintry age to feel no chill,
With me is to be lovely still,
> My Mary!

But ah! by constant heed I know
How oft the sadness that I show
Transforms thy smiles to looks of woe,
> My Mary!

And should my future lot be cast
With much resemblance of the past,
Thy worn-out heart will break at last—
> My Mary!

JAMES BEATTIE

1735–1803

472.   *An Epitaph*

L IKE thee I once have stemm'd the sea of life,
  Like thee have languish'd after empty joys,
Like thee have labour'd in the stormy strife,
    Been grieved for trifles, and amused with toys.

Forget my frailties; thou art also frail:
    Forgive my lapses; for thyself may'st fall:
Nor read unmoved my artless tender tale—
    I was a friend, O man, to thee, to all.

ISOBEL PAGAN

1740–1821

473.   *Ca' the Yowes to the Knowes*

C A' the yowes to the knowes,
  Ca' them where the heather grows,
Ca' them where the burnie rows,
    My bonnie dearie.

As I gaed down the water side,
There I met my shepherd lad;
He row'd me sweetly in his plaid,
    And he ca'd me his dearie.

'Will ye gang down the water side,
And see the waves sae sweetly glide
Beneath the hazels spreading wide?
    The moon it shines fu' clearly.'

473. yowes] ewes.   knowes] knolls, little hills.
rows] rolls.   row'd] rolled, wrapped.

'I was bred up at nae sic school,
  My shepherd lad, to play the fool,
  And a' the day to sit in dool,
      And naebody to see me.'

'Ye sall get gowns and ribbons meet,
  Cauf-leather shoon upon your feet,
  And in my arms ye'se lie and sleep,
      And ye sall be my dearie.'

'If ye'll but stand to what ye've said,
  I'se gang wi' you, my shepherd lad,
  And ye may row me in your plaid,
      And I sall be your dearie.'

'While waters wimple to the sea,
  While day blinks in the lift sae hie,
  Till clay-cauld death sall blin' my e'e,
      Ye aye sall be my dearie!'

ANNA LÆTITIA BARBAULD

1743–1825

474.   *Life*

L IFE! I know not what thou art,
  But know that thou and I must part;
And when, or how, or where we met,
I own to me 's a secret yet.
But this I know, when thou art fled,
Where'er they lay these limbs, this head,
No clod so valueless shall be
As all that then remains of me.

O whither, whither dost thou fly?
Where bend unseen thy trackless course?

473. dool] dule, sorrow.   lift] sky.

And in this strange divorce,
Ah, tell where I must seek this compound I?
To the vast ocean of empyreal flame
From whence thy essence came
Dost thou thy flight pursue, when freed
From matter's base encumbering weed?
Or dost thou, hid from sight,
Wait, like some spell-bound knight,
Through blank oblivious years th' appointed hour
To break thy trance and reassume thy power?
Yet canst thou without thought or feeling be?
O say, what art thou, when no more thou'rt thee?

Life! we have been long together,
Through pleasant and through cloudy weather;
'Tis hard to part when friends are dear;
Perhaps 'twill cost a sigh, a tear;—
Then steal away, give little warning,
Choose thine own time;
Say not Good-night, but in some brighter clime
Bid me Good-morning!

FANNY GREVILLE

18th Century

475.   *Prayer for Indifference*

I ASK no kind return of love,
   No tempting charm to please;
Far from the heart those gifts remove,
   That sighs for peace and ease.

Nor peace nor ease the heart can know,
   That, like the needle true,
Turns at the touch of joy or woe,
   But turning, trembles too.

FANNY GREVILLE

Far as distress the soul can wound,
  'Tis pain in each degree:
'Tis bliss but to a certain bound,
  Beyond is agony.

JOHN LOGAN

1748–1788

476.   *To the Cuckoo*

HAIL, beauteous stranger of the grove!
    Thou messenger of Spring!
Now Heaven repairs thy rural seat,
  And woods thy welcome ring.

What time the daisy decks the green,
  Thy certain voice we hear:
Hast thou a star to guide thy path,
  Or mark the rolling year?

Delightful visitant! with thee
  I hail the time of flowers,
And hear the sound of music sweet
  From birds among the bowers.

The schoolboy, wand'ring through the wood
  To pull the primrose gay,
Starts, the new voice of Spring to hear,
  And imitates thy lay.

What time the pea puts on the bloom,
  Thou fli'st thy vocal vale,
An annual guest in other lands,
  Another Spring to hail.

Sweet bird! thy bower is ever green,
  Thy sky is ever clear;
Thou hast no sorrow in thy song,
  No Winter in thy year!

226

O could I fly, I'd fly with thee!
 We'd make, with joyful wing,
Our annual visit o'er the globe,
 Companions of the Spring.

LADY ANNE LINDSAY

1750–1825

477.   *Auld Robin Gray*

WHEN the sheep are in the fauld, and the kye at hame,
 And a' the warld to rest are gane,
The waes o' my heart fa' in showers frae my e'e,
While my gudeman lies sound by me.

Young Jamie lo'ed me weel, and sought me for his bride;
But saving a croun he had naething else beside:
To make the croun a pund, young Jamie gaed to sea;
And the croun and the pund were baith for me.

He hadna been awa' a week but only twa,
When my father brak his arm, and the cow was stown awa';
My mother she fell sick,—and my Jamie at the sea—
And auld Robin Gray came a-courtin' me.

My father couldna work, and my mother couldna spin;
I toil'd day and night, but their bread I couldna win;
Auld Rob maintain'd them baith, and wi' tears in his e'e
Said, 'Jennie, for their sakes, O, marry me!'

My heart it said nay; I look'd for Jamie back;
But the wind it blew high, and the ship it was a wrack;
His ship it was a wrack—Why didna Jamie dee?
Or why do I live to cry, Wae's me?

My father urged me sair: my mother didna speak;
But she look'd in my face till my heart was like to break:
They gi'ed him my hand, tho' my heart was in the sea;
Sae auld Robin Gray he was gudeman to me.

I hadna been a wife a week but only four,
When mournfu' as I sat on the stane at the door,
I saw my Jamie's wraith,—for I couldna think it he,
Till he said, 'I'm come hame to marry thee.'

O sair, sair did we greet, and muckle did we say;
We took but ae kiss, and we tore ourselves away:
I wish that I were dead, but I'm no like to dee;
And why was I born to say, Wae's me!

I gang like a ghaist, and I carena to spin;
I daurna think on Jamie, for that wad be a sin;
But I'll do my best a gude wife aye to be,
For auld Robin Gray he is kind unto me.

SIR WILLIAM JONES

1746–1794

478. *Epigram*

ON parent knees, a naked new-born child,
    Weeping thou sat'st while all around thee smiled:
So live, that sinking to thy life's last sleep,
Calm thou may'st smile, whilst all around thee weep.

THOMAS CHATTERTON

1752–1770

479. *Song from Ælla*

O SING unto my roundelay,
    O drop the briny tear with me;
Dance no more at holyday,
Like a running river be:
        My love is dead,
        Gone to his death-bed
All under the willow-tree.

THOMAS CHATTERTON

Black his cryne as the winter night,
White his rode as the summer snow,
Red his face as the morning light,
Cold he lies in the grave below:
    My love is dead,
      Gone to his death-bed
All under the willow-tree.

Sweet his tongue as the throstle's note,
Quick in dance as thought can be,
Deft his tabor, cudgel stout;
O he lies by the willow-tree!
    My love is dead,
      Gone to his death-bed
All under the willow-tree.

Hark! the raven flaps his wing
In the brier'd dell below;
Hark! the death-owl loud doth sing
To the nightmares, as they go:
    My love is dead,
      Gone to his death-bed
All under the willow-tree.

See! the white moon shines on high;
Whiter is my true-love's shroud:
Whiter than the morning sky,
Whiter than the evening cloud:
    My love is dead,
      Gone to his death-bed
All under the willow-tree.

Here upon my true-love's grave
Shall the barren flowers be laid;
Not one holy saint to save
All the coldness of a maid:

cryne] hair.   rode] complexion.

My love is dead,
　　Gone to his death-bed
All under the willow-tree.

With my hands I'll dent the briers
Round his holy corse to gre:
Ouph and fairy, light your fires,
Here my body still shall be:
　　My love is dead,
　　Gone to his death-bed
All under the willow-tree.

Come, with acorn-cup and thorn,
Drain my heartés blood away;
Life and all its good I scorn,
Dance by night, or feast by day:
　　My love is dead,
　　Gone to his death-bed
All under the willow-tree.

GEORGE CRABBE

1754–1832

480.　　　　　*Meeting*

MY Damon was the first to wake
　　The gentle flame that cannot die;
My Damon is the last to take
　　The faithful bosom's softest sigh:
The life between is nothing worth,
　　O cast it from thy thought away!
Think of the day that gave it birth,
　　And this its sweet returning day.

479. dent] fast.　gre] grow.　ouph] elf.

Buried be all that has been done,
    Or say that naught is done amiss;
For who the dangerous path can shun
    In such bewildering world as this?
But love can every fault forgive,
    Or with a tender look reprove;
And now let naught in memory live
    But that we meet, and that we love.

481.   *Late Wisdom*

WE'VE trod the maze of error round,
    Long wandering in the winding glade;
And now the torch of truth is found,
    It only shows us where we strayed:
By long experience taught, we know—
    Can rightly judge of friends and foes;
Can all the worth of these allow,
    And all the faults discern in those.

Now, 'tis our boast that we can quell
    The wildest passions in their rage,
Can their destructive force repel,
    And their impetuous wrath assuage.—
Ah, Virtue! dost thou arm when now
    This bold rebellious race are fled?
When all these tyrants rest, and thou
    Art warring with the mighty dead?

482.   *A Marriage Ring*

THE ring, so worn as you behold,
    So thin, so pale, is yet of gold:
The passion such it was to prove—
Worn with life's care, love yet was love.

WILLIAM BLAKE

1757–1827

483.   *To the Muses*

WHETHER on Ida's shady brow
    Or in the chambers of the East,
The chambers of the Sun, that now
    From ancient melody have ceased;

Whether in heaven ye wander fair,
    Or the green corners of the earth,
Or the blue regions of the air
    Where the melodious winds have birth;

Whether on crystal rocks ye rove,
    Beneath the bosom of the sea,
Wandering in many a coral grove;
    Fair Nine, forsaking Poetry;

How have you left the ancient love
    That bards of old enjoy'd in you!
The languid strings do scarcely move,
    The sound is forced, the notes are few.

484.   *To Spring*

O THOU with dewy locks, who lookest down
    Through the clear windows of the morning, turn
Thine angel eyes upon our western isle,
Which in full choir hails thy approach, O Spring!

The hills tell one another, and the listening
Valleys hear; all our longing eyes are turn'd
Up to thy bright pavilions: issue forth
And let thy holy feet visit our clime!

Come o'er the eastern hills, and let our winds
Kiss thy perfuméd garments; let us taste
Thy morn and evening breath; scatter thy pearls
Upon our lovesick land that mourns for thee.

O deck her forth with thy fair fingers; pour
Thy soft kisses on her bosom; and put
Thy golden crown upon her languish'd head,
Whose modest tresses are bound up for thee.

485.   *Song*

M Y silks and fine array,
    My smiles and languish'd air,
By Love are driven away;
    And mournful lean Despair
Brings me yew to deck my grave:
Such end true lovers have.

His face is fair as heaven
    When springing buds unfold:
O why to him was 't given,
    Whose heart is wintry cold?
His breast is Love's all-worshipp'd tomb,
Where all Love's pilgrims come.

Bring me an axe and spade,
    Bring me a winding-sheet;
When I my grave have made,
    Let winds and tempests beat:
Then down I'll lie, as cold as clay:
True love doth pass away!

486.   *Reeds of Innocence*

PIPING down the valleys wild,
    Piping songs of pleasant glee,
On a cloud I saw a child,
    And he laughing said to me:

'Pipe a song about a Lamb!'
    So I piped with merry cheer.
'Piper, pipe that song again;'
    So I piped: he wept to hear.

'Drop thy pipe, thy happy pipe;
    Sing thy songs of happy cheer!'
So I sung the same again,
    While he wept with joy to hear.

'Piper, sit thee down and write
    In a book that all may read.'
So he vanish'd from my sight;
    And I pluck'd a hollow reed,

And I made a rural pen,
    And I stain'd the water clear,
And I wrote my happy songs
    Every child may joy to hear.

487.   *The Little Black Boy*

MY mother bore me in the southern wild,
    And I am black, but O, my soul is white!
White as an angel is the English child,
    But I am black, as if bereaved of light.

My mother taught me underneath a tree,
    And, sitting down before the heat of day,
She took me on her lap and kisséd me,
    And, pointing to the East, began to say:

'Look at the rising sun: there God does live,
    And gives His light, and gives His heat away,
And flowers and trees and beasts and men receive
    Comfort in morning, joy in the noonday.

'And we are put on earth a little space,
    That we may learn to bear the beams of love;
And these black bodies and this sunburnt face
    Are but a cloud, and like a shady grove.

'For when our souls have learn'd the heat to bear,
    The cloud will vanish; we shall hear His voice,
Saying, "Come out from the grove, my love and care,
    And round my golden tent like lambs rejoice." '

Thus did my mother say, and kisséd me,
    And thus I say to little English boy.
When I from black and he from white cloud free,
    And round the tent of God like lambs we joy,

I'll shade him from the heat till he can bear
    To lean in joy upon our Father's knee;
And then I'll stand and stroke his silver hair,
    And be like him, and he will then love me.

488. *Hear the Voice*

HEAR the voice of the Bard,
    Who present, past, and future, sees;
Whose ears have heard
The Holy Word
That walk'd among the ancient trees;

Calling the lapséd soul,
    And weeping in the evening dew;
That might control
The starry pole,
And fallen, fallen light renew!

'O Earth, O Earth, return!
Arise from out the dewy grass!
Night is worn,
And the morn
Rises from the slumbrous mass.

'Turn away no more;
Why wilt thou turn away?
The starry floor,
The watery shore,
Is given thee till the break of day.'

489.   *The Tiger*

TIGER, tiger, burning bright
In the forests of the night,
What immortal hand or eye
Could frame thy fearful symmetry?

In what distant deeps or skies
Burnt the fire of thine eyes?
On what wings dare he aspire?
What the hand dare seize the fire?

And what shoulder and what art
Could twist the sinews of thy heart?
And, when thy heart began to beat,
What dread hand and what dread feet?

What the hammer? what the chain?
In what furnace was thy brain?
What the anvil? What dread grasp
Dare its deadly terrors clasp?

When the stars threw down their spears,
And water'd heaven with their tears,
Did He smile His work to see?
Did He who made the lamb make thee?

Tiger, tiger, burning bright
In the forests of the night,
What immortal hand or eye
Dare frame thy fearful symmetry?

490. *Cradle Song*

SLEEP, sleep, beauty bright,
 Dreaming in the joys of night;
Sleep, sleep; in thy sleep
Little sorrows sit and weep.

Sweet babe, in thy face
Soft desires I can trace,
Secret joys and secret smiles,
Little pretty infant wiles.

As thy softest limbs I feel
Smiles as of the morning steal
O'er thy cheek, and o'er thy breast
Where thy little heart doth rest.

O the cunning wiles that creep
In thy little heart asleep!
When thy little heart doth wake,
Then the dreadful night shall break.

491. *Night*

THE sun descending in the west,
 The evening star does shine;
The birds are silent in their nest.
 And I must seek for mine.
  The moon, like a flower
  In heaven's high bower,
  With silent delight
  Sits and smiles on the night.

Farewell, green fields and happy grove,
    Where flocks have took delight:
Where lambs have nibbled, silent move
    The feet of angels bright;
        Unseen they pour blessing
        And joy without ceasing
        On each bud and blossom,
        And each sleeping bosom.

They look in every thoughtless nest
    Where birds are cover'd warm;
They visit caves of every beast,
    To keep them all from harm:
        If they see any weeping
        That should have been sleeping,
        They pour sleep on their head,
        And sit down by their bed.

When wolves and tigers howl for prey,
    They pitying stand and weep,
Seeking to drive their thirst away
    And keep them from the sheep.
        But, if they rush dreadful,
        The angels, most heedful,
        Receive each mild spirit,
        New worlds to inherit.

And there the lion's ruddy eyes
    Shall flow with tears of gold:
And pitying the tender cries,
    And walking round the fold:
        Saying, 'Wrath, by His meekness,
        And, by His health, sickness,
        Are driven away
        From our immortal day.

'And now beside thee, bleating lamb,
   I can lie down and sleep,
Or think on Him who bore thy name,
   Graze after thee, and weep.
     For, wash'd in life's river,
     My bright mane for ever
     Shall shine like the gold
     As I guard o'er the fold.'

492.   *Love's Secret*

NEVER seek to tell thy love,
   Love that never told can be;
For the gentle wind doth move
   Silently, invisibly.

I told my love, I told my love,
   I told her all my heart,
Trembling, cold, in ghastly fears.
   Ah! she did depart!

Soon after she was gone from me,
   A traveller came by,
Silently, invisibly:
   He took her with a sigh.

ROBERT BURNS

1759–1796

493.   *Mary Morison*

O MARY, at thy window be,
    It is the wish'd, the trysted hour!
Those smiles and glances let me see,
    That make the miser's treasure poor:
How blythely wad I bide the stour
    A weary slave frae sun to sun,
Could I the rich reward secure,
    The lovely Mary Morison!

Yestreen, when to the trembling string
    The dance gaed thro' the lighted ha',
To thee my fancy took its wing,
    I sat, but neither heard nor saw:
Tho' this was fair, and that was braw,
    And yon the toast of a' the town,
I sigh'd, and said amang them a',
    'Ye arena Mary Morison.'

O Mary, canst thou wreck his peace,
    Wha for thy sake wad gladly die?
Or canst thou break that heart of his,
    Whase only faut is loving thee?
If love for love thou wiltna gie,
    At least be pity to me shown;
A thought ungentle canna be
    The thought o' Mary Morison.

stour] dust, turmoil.

494. *Jean*

OF a' the airts the wind can blaw,
 I dearly like the west,
For there the bonnie lassie lives,
 The lassie I lo'e best:
There wild woods grow, and rivers row,
 And monie a hill between;
But day and night my fancy's flight
 Is ever wi' my Jean.

I see her in the dewy flowers,
 I see her sweet and fair:
I hear her in the tunefu' birds,
 I hear her charm the air:
There 's not a bonnie flower that springs
 By fountain, shaw, or green;
There's not a bonnie bird that sings,
 But minds me o' my Jean.

495. *Auld Lang Syne*

SHOULD auld acquaintance be forgot,
 And never brought to min'?
Should auld acquaintance be forgot,
 And days o' lang syne?

We twa hae rin about the braes,
 And pu'd the gowans fine;
But we've wander'd monie a weary fit
 Sin' auld lang syne.

---

494. airts] points of the compass. row] roll.
495. gowans] daisies. fit] foot.

We twa hae paidl't i' the burn,
  Frae mornin' sun till dine;
But seas between us braid hae roar'd
  Sin' auld lang syne.

And here 's a hand, my trusty fiere,
  And gie's a hand o' thine;
And we'll tak a right guid-willie waught
  For auld lang syne.

And surely ye'll be your pint-stowp,
  And surely I'll be mine;
And we'll tak a cup o' kindness yet
  For auld lang syne!

    For auld lang syne, my dear,
      For auld lang syne,
    We'll tak a cup o' kindness yet
      For auld lang syne.

496.   *My Bonnie Mary*

GO fetch to me a pint o' wine,
  An' fill it in a silver tassie,
That I may drink, before I go,
  A service to my bonnie lassie.
The boat rocks at the pier o' Leith,
  Fu' loud the wind blaws frae the ferry,
The ship rides by the Berwick-law,
  And I maun leave my bonnie Mary.

The trumpets sound, the banners fly,
  The glittering spears are rankéd ready;
The shouts o' war are heard afar,
  The battle closes thick and bloody;

495. dine] dinner-time.   fiere] partner.
guid-willie waught] friendly draught.   496. tassie] cup.

But it 's no the roar o' sea or shore
    Wad mak me langer wish to tarry;
Nor shout o' war that 's heard afar—
    It 's leaving thee, my bonnie Mary!

497.   *John Anderson, My Jo*

JOHN ANDERSON, my jo, John,
    When we were first acquent,
Your locks were like the raven,
    Your bonnie brow was brent;
But now your brow is beld, John,
    Your locks are like the snow;
But blessings on your frosty pow,
    John Anderson, my jo!

John Anderson, my jo, John,
    We clamb the hill thegither;
And monie a canty day, John,
    We've had wi' ane anither:
Now we maun totter down, John,
    But hand in hand we'll go,
And sleep thegither at the foot,
    John Anderson, my jo.

498.   *The Banks o' Doon*

YE flowery banks o' bonnie Doon,
    How can ye blume sae fair!
How can ye chant, ye little birds,
    And I sae fu' o' care!

Thou'll break my heart, thou bonnie bird,
    That sings upon the bough;

497. jo] sweetheart.   brent] smooth, unwrinkled.
beld] bald.   pow] pate.   canty] cheerful.

Thou minds me o' the happy days
   When my fause luve was true.

Thou'll break my heart, thou bonnie bird,
   That sings beside thy mate;
For sae I sat, and sae I sang,
   And wistna o' my fate.

Aft hae I roved by bonnie Doon,
   To see the woodbine twine;
And ilka bird sang o' its luve,
   And sae did I o' mine.

Wi' lightsome heart I pu'd a rose
   Upon a morn in June;
And sae I flourish'd on the morn,
   And sae was pu'd or' noon.

Wi' lightsome heart I pu'd a rose
   Upon its thorny tree;
But my fause luver staw my rose,
   And left the thorn wi' me.

499.   *Ae Fond Kiss*

AE fond kiss, and then we sever;
   Ae fareweel, alas, for ever!
Deep in heart-wrung tears I'll pledge thee,
Warring sighs and groans I'll wage thee!

Who shall say that Fortune grieves him
While the star of hope she leaves him?
Me, nae cheerfu' twinkle lights me,
Dark despair around benights me.

I'll ne'er blame my partial fancy;
Naething could resist my Nancy;

498. or'] ere.   staw] stole.
499. wage] stake, plight.

But to see her was to love her,
Love but her, and love for ever.

Had we never loved sae kindly,
Had we never loved sae blindly,
Never met—or never parted,
We had ne'er been broken-hearted.

Fare thee weel, thou first and fairest!
Fare thee weel, thou best and dearest!
Thine be ilka joy and treasure,
Peace, enjoyment, love, and pleasure!

Ae fond kiss, and then we sever!
Ae fareweel, alas, for ever!
Deep in heart-wrung tears I'll pledge thee,
Warring sighs and groans I'll wage thee!

500. *Bonnie Lesley*

O saw ye bonnie Lesley
    As she gaed o'er the Border?
She 's gane, like Alexander,
    To spread her conquests farther.

To see her is to love her,
    And love but her for ever;
For Nature made her what she is,
    And ne'er made sic anither!

Thou art a queen, fair Lesley,
    Thy subjects we, before thee:
Thou art divine, fair Lesley,
    The hearts o' men adore thee.

The Deil he couldna scaith thee,
    Or aught that wad belang thee;

500. scaith] harm.

He'd look into thy bonnie face
    And say, 'I canna wrang thee!'

The Powers aboon will tent thee,
    Misfortune sha'na steer thee:
Thou'rt like themsel' sae lovely,
    That ill they'll ne'er let near thee.

Return again, fair Lesley,
    Return to Caledonie!
That we may brag we hae a lass
    There 's nane again sae bonnie!

501.   *Highland Mary*

YE banks and braes and streams around
    The castle o' Montgomery,
Green be your woods, and fair your flowers,
    Your waters never drumlie!
There simmer first unfauld her robes,
    And there the langest tarry;
For there I took the last fareweel
    O' my sweet Highland Mary.

How sweetly bloom'd the gay green birk,
    How rich the hawthorn's blossom,
As underneath their fragrant shade
    I clasp'd her to my bosom!
The golden hours on angel wings
    Flew o'er me and my dearie;
For dear to me as light and life
    Was my sweet Highland Mary.

Wi' monie a vow and lock'd embrace
    Our parting was fu' tender;

500. tent] watch.   steer] molest.
501. drumlie] miry.

And, pledging aft to meet again,
　　We tore oursels asunder;
But oh! fell Death's untimely frost,
　　That nipt my flower sae early!
Now green 's the sod, and cauld 's the clay,
　　That wraps my Highland Mary!

O pale, pale now, those rosy lips
　　I aft hae kiss'd sae fondly!
And closed for aye the sparkling glance
　　That dwelt on me sae kindly!
And mouldering now in silent dust
　　That heart that lo'ed me dearly!
But still within my bosom's core
　　Shall live my Highland Mary.

502.　*O Were My Love Yon Lilac Fair*

O WERE my Love yon lilac fair,
　　Wi' purple blossoms to the spring,
And I a bird to shelter there,
　　When wearied on my little wing;
How I wad mourn when it was torn
　　By autumn wild and winter rude!
But I wad sing on wanton wing
　　When youthfu' May its bloom renew'd.

O gin my Love were yon red rose
　　That grows upon the castle wa',
And I mysel a drap o' dew,
　　Into her bonnie breast to fa';
O there, beyond expression blest,
　　I'd feast on beauty a' the night;
Seal'd on her silk-saft faulds to rest,
　　Till fley'd awa' by Phœbus' light.

503. *A Red, Red Rose*

O MY Luve 's like a red, red rose
　　That's newly sprung in June:
O my Luve 's like the melodie
　　That 's sweetly play'd in tune!

As fair art thou, my bonnie lass,
　　So deep in luve am I:
And I will luve thee still, my dear,
　　Till a' the seas gang dry:

Till a' the seas gang dry, my dear,
　　And the rocks melt wi' the sun;
I will luve thee still, my dear,
　　While the sands o' life shall run.

And fare thee weel, my only Luve,
　　And fare thee weel a while!
And I will come again, my Luve,
　　Tho' it were ten thousand mile.

504. *Lament for Culloden*

THE lovely lass o' Inverness,
　　Nae joy nor pleasure can she see;
For e'en and morn she cries, 'Alas!'
　　And aye the saut tear blin's her e'e:
'Drumossie moor, Drumossie day,
　　A waefu' day it was to me!
For there I lost my father dear,
　　My father dear and brethren three.

'Their winding-sheet the bluidy clay,
　　Their graves are growing green to see;
And by them lies the dearest lad
　　That ever blest a woman's e'e!

Now wae to thee, thou cruel lord,
A bluidy man I trow thou be;
For monie a heart thou hast made sair,
That ne'er did wrang to thine or thee.'

505.   *The Farewell*

IT was a' for our rightfu' King
We left fair Scotland's strand;
It was a' for our rightfu' King
We e'er saw Irish land,
My dear—
We e'er saw Irish land.

Now a' is done that men can do,
And a' is done in vain;
My love and native land, farewell,
For I maun cross the main,
My dear—
For I maun cross the main.

He turn'd him right and round about
Upon the Irish shore;
And gae his bridle-reins a shake,
With, Adieu for evermore,
My dear—
With, Adieu for evermore!

The sodger frae the wars returns,
The sailor frae the main;
But I hae parted frae my love,
Never to meet again,
My dear—
Never to meet again.

When day is gane, and night is come,
And a' folk bound to sleep,

I think on him that 's far awa',
　　The lee-lang night, and weep,
　　　　My dear—
　　The lee-lang night, and weep.

506.　　　　*Hark!　The Mavis*

C*A' the yowes to the knowes,*
　Ca' them where the heather grows,
Ca' them where the burnie rows,
　My bonnie dearie.

Hark! the mavis' evening sang
Sounding Clouden's woods amang,
Then a-faulding let us gang,
　　My bonnie dearie.

We'll gae down by Clouden side,
Through the hazels spreading wide,
O'er the waves that sweetly glide
　　To the moon sae clearly.

Yonder Clouden's silent towers,
Where at moonshine midnight hours
O'er the dewy bending flowers
　　Fairies dance sae cheery.

Ghaist nor bogle shalt thou fear;
Thou'rt to Love and Heaven sae dear,
Nocht of ill may come thee near,
　　My bonnie dearie.

Fair and lovely as thou art,
Thou hast stown my very heart;
I can die—but canna part,
　　My bonnie dearie.

505. lee-lang] livelong.

While waters wimple to the sea;
While day blinks in the lift sae hie;
Till clay-cauld death shall blin' my e'e,
    Ye shall be my dearie.

Ca' the yowes to the knowes . . .

lift] sky.

CPSIA information can be obtained
at www.ICGtesting.com
Printed in the USA
BVHW071659200721
612415BV00007B/332